The 25th

New and Selected Christmas Essays

by Joshua Gibbs

CiRCE
Concord, NC

Published in the USA
by the CiRCE Institute
@2020 Joshua Gibbs
ISBN: 978-1-7347853-4-0

All rights reserved. This publication may not be reproduced, stored in a retrieval system, or transmitted, in any form or by any means, without the prior written permission of the CiRCE Institute.

For information:
CiRCE Institute
81 McCachern Blvd.
Concord, NC 28025
www.circeinstitute.org

Cover design by Graeme Pitman
Layout by Courtney Sanford

Printed in the United States of America.

For Camilla and Beatrice

"Born that man no more may die."
—Charles Wesley

"I want to wish you a Merry Christmas from the bottom of my heart."
—José Feliciano

Acknowledgements

My desire to write in defense of Christmas began six years ago when my family took a trip to the Willow Oak Christmas Tree Farm in Woodford, Virginia. The gentleman who owns the farm invites customers to enter his home and take in the spectacle of a miniature Christmas village he sets up annually in the foyer. The village is sprawling, contains many thousands of pieces, and represents not only a great financial investment, but an even greater investment of time, space, and labor. From the moment I saw the village, it struck me not as a hobby, but as a beautiful and meticulous homage to the Incarnation. I wanted to imitate this man's love of Christmas.

Table of Contents

Introduction: On Grinches i

A Better World 1

In Defense of Santa Claus 15

When to Start Listening to Christmas Music 35

In Defense of George Bailey 45

Meditations on the Creche 53

What if Christmas Is Exactly What It Purports to Be? 97

Death at a Party 135
December 28th, Feast of the Holy Innocents

The Leavetaking 141

Bibliography 151

Introduction

On Grinches

Everyone loves Christmas. Everyone except grinches. Of course, there are atheists who think Christmas a needlessly religious holiday and believe that "Be good for goodness' sake" is more compelling than "Be good for Christ's sake," which only complicates the matter of morality for a pluralist society. Such atheists enjoy catchy, godless Christmas pop songs, fudge, and the marriage of colors red and green just as much as Catholics do, but would prefer Christmas to merely be a time of humanistic goodwill and the enjoyment of seasonally winterish foods and clothing. Such atheists do not love Christmas, but they are not grinches.

Likewise, there is a very small sect of Presbyterians yet populating the planet who believe that Christmas is nothing more than a Catholic superstition and that Scripture never commands us to celebrate it, which means we are free to do what we please on December 25. As much as I love Christmas, I cannot fault this small sect for clinging faithfully to the sixteenth-century roots of their church. They are, in fact, good traditionalists who respect John Knox—and, besides, it is out of respect for tradition that I celebrate Christmas. These people are not grinches, at least not in my book.

The grinch is a curious creature who does not oppose Christmas on religious grounds, as do the atheist and the very traditional Presbyterian. The grinch is almost certainly a baptized Christian, may attend nearly any church present in North America, and, during the month of July or August, seems a perfectly normal human being who pays his tithes and his taxes, does not drink too much, mows his own lawn, and so forth. And yet, come late November, the grinch recalls his great distaste for Christmas. He neither enjoys nor trusts Christmas, though he knows most people do. Much of the time, his dislike of Christmas is hidden, for he knows it is uncouth to complain about Christmas, given how most people feel about it. He does not campaign against Christmas, does not refrain from giving gifts, does not sabotage the children's Christmas pageant. However, from time to time, he throws an unironic "Ba humbug" into the midst of others' Christmas plans and then sulkily leaves the room.

I suppose we could call such people "scrooges," although both "scrooge" and "grinch" make awkward sobriquets for people who do not like Christmas given that, by the end of their respective stories, both Seuss' Grinch and Dickens' Scrooge have become great champions of Christmas. I think "grinch" a better title for the modern man who does not like Christmas because his distaste for Christmas is more in keeping with Seuss's villain than Dickens'. At the beginning of *A Christmas Carol*, Scrooge hates Christmas because he is greedy and despises all the petitions for charity which beset him during Advent. On the other hand, Seuss's Grinch hates Christmas for idealistic reasons. He believes Christmas is crass, self-indulgent, and materialistic, and endeavors to rub all the Whos' noses in this embarrassing fact by stealing their feasts and their gifts.

I would wager that every church in America with more than a hundred parishioners has at least one grinch. Almost all grinches are men—fathers, in fact—who believe that Christmas is nothing more than a cash grab, perhaps even the kind of cash grab which is "run by a big Eastern syndicate," as Lucy says in *A Charlie Brown Christmas*. When these men watch *How the Grinch Stole Christmas!* they secretly pity the Grinch, for they know his loathing of Christmas is right, and that the ending of the film, wherein the Whos blithely dismiss the theft of their feasts and gifts and gather in the town square to sing, is nothing more than Christmas propaganda which unjustly dismisses the Grinch's concerns and moronically assumes that man is good. Did the Whos not see their things were stolen? Did they not care? Did none of them think to call the police, at very least? Is the dismissive response of the Whos to the sanctity of their homes being violated by burglars not evidence they are a few balls short of a decorated tree? Besides this, the grinch has heard that Jesus Christ was not actually born on December 25 and so he not only views Christmas as a grubby cash grab, but an arbitrary one that drags on many weeks too long. The goodwill, generosity, and cheer typically associated with Christmas are nothing more than a pious façade with which to disguise the brutal heart and soul of the fiscal year, those thirty or so days by which thousands of American businesses live or die.

 I shall need the long haul of this book to address all of the grinch's concerns, though I should begin by pointing out that most grinches are men because women are simply too busy with the work of Christmas to make ideological complaints about it. Men object that the Christmas season is too long; however, it is typically women who unpack the Christmas decorations, arrange them tastefully around the house, purchase presents for aunts and uncles and godmothers, wrap those presents, take the presents to the post office, bake (and gift wrap) banana bread for their children's teachers and the priest and the whole Sunday school, find out what the children want for Christmas, and make Christmas cards, the last of which is no longer a simple task, but now a presentation of the family's character, taste, and social status to the watching world. The man's part in preparing for Christmas is far smaller, though, and often concerns little more than acquiring the tree, perhaps by obtaining a license from the state to cut it down from the woods, but probably by purchasing one (that is already netted) from a grocery store parking lot. Of course, it may very well be that the man's part in Christmas is simply to bankroll all the aforementioned activities, and I am not making any sort of claim about the unfairness of gender roles or suggesting women should revolt against the Christmas-oriented work which falls to them during December. I am simply pointing out that those who spend a good bit of their time on Christmas rarely think the time is wasted. "Ba humbug" is not something one says while mopping his brow.

More importantly, though, it must be noted that grinches are not born, but made. No child hates Christmas, which means that every grinch must recall the point at which he passed from a childlike love of the holiday to a geriatric hatred of it—for though some grinches are only middle-aged, the hatred of Christmas is clearly an old man's complaint. One cannot listen to a grinch's diatribe against Christmas without recalling Aristotle's description of the elderly: "They have lived many years; they have often been taken in, and often made mistakes; and life on the whole is a bad business. . . . They are small-minded, because they have been humbled by life. . . . They are not generous, because money is one of the things they must have, and at the same time their experience has taught them how hard it is to get and how easy to lose."[1] Between the childlike love of Christmas and the grinch's disgust, we may intuit a middle ground, whereby the grinch passes through some uncertainty about the nature of Christmas. The grinch is a cynic and cynicism is born of disappointed

---

1.1 Aristotle, *Rhetoric*, 85.

love, not primal hatred. The most cynical atheists are former Christians whose love and confidence in the church slowly eroded before collapsing. The most deeply cynical critics of American public schools usually have years of teaching experience under their belts. The course of events whereby cynics are made involves institutional failure—or, the perception of it—but the accusation of institutional failure is often prefaced by years of personal failure during which the one slated for cynicism blames himself. After blaming himself for so long, he finally comes to blame the institution and exonerates himself. Cynicism always involves self-justification.

How does Christmas fail the grinch, then? Or, how does the grinch fail Christmas?

To answer this question, it will be helpful to note that *A Christmas Carol* and *How the Grinch Stole Christmas!* were written a little more than a hundred years apart, the former in 1843 and the latter in 1957. In the middle of the nineteenth century, Scrooge was angered by all those who came to him begging alms. In the middle of the twentieth century, the Grinch is vexed by the consumerism and materialism he sees during the Christmas season. Their frustrations could not be more different. Just a few years before *The Grinch* was released, C. S. Lewis penned "Xmas and Christmas:

A Lost Chapter from Herodotus"[2] in which he also complained about how commercial Christmas had become and contended there was some older, truer celebration of Christmas that had been lost to time. Eight years after *The Grinch* was released, *A Charlie Brown Christmas* once more mocked the commercialism of Christmas, while also suggesting a pure and undefiled celebration of the holiday was possible. Suffice to say, in the several decades which followed World War II, complaining about the commercialism of Christmas became a very fashionable and noble thing to do.

Compare thoughts on Christmas which were popular (or coming from geniuses the likes of Lewis) in the 1950s and 1960s with the cultural institution of Christmas in the fifty years beforehand, by which I mean, "Yes, Virginia, There Is A Santa Claus," *Miracle on 34th Street*, and *It's a Wonderful Life*. There is not so much as a hint of cynicism about Christmas in such movies. Tracing the history of Christmas, one finds that accusations of commercialism are relatively recent, even if Protestants of the sixteenth and seventeenth centuries commonly accused Catholics of using Christmas as an excuse to get drunk. At the time,

---

[2] This essay is contained in Lewis's well-known anthology *God in the Dock* (Eerdmans, 1970)

nothing like commercialism existed, for commercialism is really a novelty of the twentieth century which emerged in the aftermath of the automobile, the lightbulb, the transistor radio, and the emergence of "popular culture." The Grinch's complaint with the Whos, after all, is not that they are wasted before the bells ring on the 25th. Rather, his complaint is timely—dated, even. The Grinch cringes over advertisements, jingles, Black Friday, extended hours, and so forth.

For as much as I like C. S. Lewis, I chalk his skepticism about Christmas up to his dislike of children, a significant personality fault which he openly admitted—for, as I will argue in later chapters, Christmas is a children's holiday: a holiday which centers around a child, the Christ child, and for which children are (to this day) the most immediate and obvious beneficiaries. Nonetheless, I do not believe that the accusations of commercialism at Christmas are entirely unfounded, but that they are obliquely true, though they miss the mark. Christmas is most certainly a very old holiday, a traditional holiday—a Roman holiday, even, and I make that remark unapologetically as an Orthodox Christian—and in order to celebrate Christmas properly, one must celebrate it in the traditional style, which necessarily involves some kind of renunciation, some kind of asceticism, during Advent. If we have become cynical about Christmas, it is because we have not properly prepared our hearts for it during Advent, and we have waltzed into the birth of Christ expecting to care about an abstract theological fact without offering any personal sacrifice to obtain it.

Simply put, the average American Christian begins celebrating Christmas the day after Thanksgiving. He eats and drinks festally though the festival is more than a month away. By the time December 25 rolls around, he is quite sick of Christmas. Nothing changes on Christmas Day, and yet he is told he should feel differently when he wakes in the morning—more joyful, more content in his religion. But why should he feel differently on the 25th than the 22nd? Or the 23rd? Accordingly, on December 26th, he feels a great mystery has come near him and yet missed him, perhaps even dodged him, and he wonders at his own misery. He becomes despondent, confused. After several consecutive Christmases spent accusing himself of impiety, he slowly becomes the Grinch and accuses Christmas itself of letting him down. He has heard all the criticisms of Christmas, the accusations it is nothing more than a game, a fraud, and yet he has cautiously persisted in his childlike faith that Christmas is what it purports to be, the timely celebration of Christ's birth. However, after many years of morbid introspection on December 26, he concludes the critics are right and that the common conception of the holiday as a good and jolly thing is entirely wrong. Perhaps Christmas was good at some point in the past, back before the capitalists and advertising executives took over, but now has become tawdry, self-serving, and deceptive.

As one who loves Christmas, I pity the man who does not love it, because I know well that good thing of which he is deprived. My intention in writing this book is not to rescue Christmas from the commercialists, the capitalists, and the economists, for they have never held Christmas captive at all, but to rescue Christmas from all those charlatans who claim that the commercialists and capitalists actually have the power to ruin the holiday, which is balderdash, for Christmas is beyond ruining. I contend that reports of the commercialization of Christmas are greatly exaggerated and that the common man is much abused in his celebration of Christ's birth, for he is told all manner of lies about Saturnalia, early Christian jealousy for pagan feasts, and Christ being born "sometime in August or September," even though there is not a shred of credible evidence in favor of such risible, self-assured claims. The Christmas cynic once believed Christmas was a miracle and this is enough to make me like him, side with him even, and I will take his cynicism as a principled stand in favor of Christmas which has simply been misguided on a few key points.

I also write for that man who has always loved Christmas but worries every year that he is being lied to, even nobly lied to, and whose celebration of Christmas is always tinged by a fear that someone is pulling one over on him. As somebody who also loves Christmas, I want this man to celebrate Christmas with simplicity of heart, unworried by all those grinches and Scrooges who chide him with their needless nitpicking and ersatz concern for "purity."

Finally, I write as one who has many good memories of Christmas from his own childhood, and who is presently the father of little children, and who believes Dostoyevsky's claim that the greatest gift parents can give their children is that of good memories. I am immensely grateful to my own parents for all the fine Christmas memories they have given me, as these memories hold a unique and potent place in my mind when I consider the value of the past. I believe there is a good and right way to celebrate Christmas, but I have no novel theories on how this should be done. Rather, I think history and tradition are reliable witnesses in sussing out the right celebration of the holiday, and as opposed to reinventing the wheel, I think we should look to our ancestors.

I hope the essays in this book will enliven your celebration of Christmas. For those parents whose children are still at home, I pray these pages will embolden your memories, that you will have the courage to remember the past with generosity and gratitude and nostalgic fear, and that your own children are the greatest beneficiaries of whatever truth I light on.

A Better World

Part I

Suppose we were *not* alone in the universe.

We are not alone, of course, for the deeps of space are filled with angels, archangels, cherubim, seraphim, and every other order of bodiless power known to Christian cosmology. But what if there were another planet in our galaxy that was occupied by beings who, like ourselves, had established their own particular way of doing things, their own culture, and their own traditions? Let us suppose there is such a place and that despite all of our faults, these beings enjoy travelling to our planet every year and staying for about five weeks.

During their stay, suppose they have the curious habit of transforming our culture so that it mirrors their own.

And suppose they do not keep to themselves but settle everywhere among us, in major cities and small rural towns alike. Like us, some of them are urbane and cosmopolitan, while others are unsophisticated and provincial. Some are rich and some poor. Their rich settle among our rich and their poor settle among our poor. Their rich and their poor live in communion with one another and over time, they develop the curious power of perfectly adapting to every aspect of life on earth, every walk of life, every nationality, every income level, every level of good or bad taste. The word has become unfashionable of late, but they really are *colonizers*.

During their stay, our radio stations play their music, our theaters run their films, and many of us dress as they do because we find them intriguing, knowing. We eat differently while they are around. We read their books and even abide by their ethics. During their stay, nearly everything about our world is accommodated to suit their tastes.

The arrival of these other beings is never on precisely the same day as the year before, but typically falls somewhere during a certain week of the calendar. They sometimes arrive a little early, but never a little late. The length of their stay gradually expands, but they always suddenly and predictably leave on the same day. During their residency, many aspects of our lives carry on as usual. We still go to work, still pay the bills, still do the dishes, still conjugate irregular verbs, but nearly everything we do is touched by their style and their ethos.

Though the most cherished virtues of their culture are generosity, leniency, and humility, the works of their culture are not one-sided, but diverse. Some of their music is solemn and pious, some is plain silly. They write books for children and adults alike, but also history books, cookbooks, and theology books—however, before leaving behind the subject of their music, it ought to be noted that the theology in their hymns is more charitable, more universal, and more open-handed than the theology in our hymns. Perhaps this is because they go to church more often than we do.

We import their holidays into our own calendar, though their holidays are dazzlingly more diverse. One of their holidays celebrates the life of a man who famously loved and cared for little children, while another commemorates all the little children who died at the hands of a famous blood-thirsty tyrant. We have been celebrating their holidays for so long, though, we no longer see that they are not our own.

Their culture is unapologetically commercial, though in a way quite different from ours. They are great buyers and sellers, not because they are greedy, but because gift-giving plays a central role in the perpetuation of their civilization. Their purchases flow away from themselves. Our own buying and selling is dominated by boredom and the need to distract ourselves from death, which means the arrival of these other beings always catches us by surprise. Having spent so much money on ourselves, we have little money with which to honor others, so we make our generous colonizers guilty of our own self-inflicted (spiritual) poverty. We accuse them of being shallow and materialistic, but this is only because our own culture deeply connects the act of buying with self-knowledge and self-fulfillment. Their culture of giving lays bare our culture of selfishness, even though buying is common to both.

Part II

Over the centuries, we have become so familiar with Christmas that we now fail to notice its metaphysical peculiarities. Like the curvature of the earth or the music of the spheres, Christmas is nearly too massive to be perceived for what it really is: an autonomous, fully formed reality all its own which colonizes the Earth for a little while at the end of every year. Just as ancient men were accustomed to an angel descending from time to time to stir up the miracle-working waters of a certain pool, so modern men are accustomed to the yearly descent of Christmas, a world separate from our own which nonetheless overlays our world like a gold tapestry.

To truly appreciate the strangeness of Christmas, one must compare it with other holidays. Christmas is not a day, it is a season. There is no Fourth of July season, no Memorial Day season, no Thanksgiving season. For those who zealously follow the church calendar, there is also the season of Lent, but Lent is not a season in the same way as Christmas. Lent is a season of abstinence, of darkness, and thus more of an anti-season than a season. During Lent, Christians are asked to step back from all those things which make a season a *season*. Simply put, Lent looks forward to a death, Christ's death, and allows us to taste the negations of death while we are still alive. But Christmas looks forward to Christ's life.

Other holidays have their own special characteristics, of course. The Fourth of July is about entertainment, by which I mean fireworks. Thanksgiving is about food. Easter is about worship. Each of these holidays is about something more, but fireworks and food and worship are the separate means by which that something more is accessed. Fireworks are the sacrament of the Fourth of July, so to speak. Roasted turkey is the sacrament of Thanksgiving. Easter is not merely about worship, of course, but when one thinks of Easter, one thinks of "going to church." Most other American holidays, like Memorial Day and Labor Day, are political in nature and thus their sacrament is either time off from work or sales on goods which create stable homes, like cars, mattresses, and washing machines. However, there is not Labor Day food or Memorial Day music or Columbus Day clothing. And when Americans have an extra day off from work, they grill. The hamburger is a fitting icon for half the federal holidays on our calendar.

On the other hand, there is a Christmas version of nearly everything: Christmas music, Christmas food, Christmas drink, Christmas dress, Christmas books, Christmas movies, Christmas colors, and Christmas spices. People decorate their homes for Christmas, but also their lawns, their cars, their pets, and their churches. Stores dress up for Christmas, but there are also stores entirely devoted to selling Christmas goods. No other holiday can claim such a universal coverage of cultural artifacts. Given the peculiar spirit of generosity which possesses people during the Christmas season, one might even say there are Christmas ethics. Just as American culture contains both secular and sacred elements, so does Christmas, for Christmas is not the exclusive interest of the marketplace, the courthouse, or the nave. Christmas began in a cave, spread quickly in the time of the Roman Empire, but never really stopped reaching out further and further to encompass every conceivable aspect of life.

While children are the greatest beneficiaries of Christmas, there are Christmas movies for old people and young people, black people and white people, conservative people and progressive people, smart people and cynical people. Christmas music is just as diverse, for there are hopeful and melancholic Christmas songs, silly and serious Christmas songs, romantic and lascivious Christmas songs, patriotic and pious Christmas songs. If it is a part of life, it is represented somewhere within Christmas culture.

Nonetheless, we so thoroughly forget about Christmas for the other ten months of the year that from the standpoint of mid-Summer, Christmas seems a mere chronological outpost fixed to the end of the calendar. A full tenth of our lives are lived out under the auspices of the Christmas season, and yet, apart from the Christmas season, we more or less forget the holiday even exists. We do not eat candy canes during February. We do not listen to Christmas music in March. A red and green dress is nearly non-existent in April. Only a madman would watch *Miracle on 34th Street* in May. Regardless of its December beauty, "Hark! The Herald Angels Sing" always sounds tinny and self-conscious if we sing it in June. Given just how vast, diverse, and extensive Christmas culture is, it is rather remarkable that we set all of it aside for the rest of the year. Americans are consummate gluttons. Why do we not help ourselves to Christmas whenever we feel like it?

Or, why do we not feel like Christmas during any other time of year? Apart from Christmas, Americans are not terribly concerned with tradition, by which I mean we eat what we want, drink what we want, watch what we want, wear what we want, and listen to what we want during the other ten and a half months of the year, and yet Christmas culture is a curious exception to this rule. In July, a man born and raised in Iowa could throw a dinner party on a Friday night, serve guests German wine, English beer, and Mexican cuisine for dinner and no one would think it odd, but if he served eggnog for dessert, he would be expected to offer an explanation. If, after supper, our man from Iowa led his guests through a French card game and poured everyone Swiss liqueur, all the while playing Celtic music, when his friends drove home hours later, the husband would probably absently mutter aloud to his wife, "Why the hell did he serve eggnog?"

Part III

Christmas is one of the last widely, deeply observed traditions left in the modern world (consider just how much of the traditional wedding has been abandoned in the last fifty years), which might be why we are particularly squeamish about seeing anything related to Christmas detached from time and tossed on the undifferentiated any-way-you-want-it cultural junk heap. In agrarian societies prior to the Modern age, nearly every week of a man's life was as particular and regimented as the modern man's life is during the fourth week of December. A farmer might thatch the roof of his home with sapling branches that were only usable if they were cut down during a particular ten-day passage of the year. Any earlier and they would be too thin, any later and they would be inflexibly stiff and could not be twisted and woven tightly into place. If the farmer did not perform his work meticulously and punctually, his attic would leak, his food would rot, and his family would starve—all because he put off a task whose modern equivalent can be painlessly rescheduled a dozen times.

The finest nuances of the farmer's labor, his diet, the size of his meals, the timing of his journeys to and from market, his yearly visit to the nearest church, the sowing of seed, the harvesting of his crop—nearly every significant aspect of his life—had to be carefully planned and coordinated lest the proper time for action be lost, the opportunity squandered, and life imperiled. There are few activities which a modern man may not put off for days, for weeks. He stalls on the purchase of a new suit for months. His home falls into disrepair and remains that way for years. Besides, we get delays and extensions on contracts and deadlines. We hit the snooze alarm once, twice. In a nearly timeless state like ours, everything can wait and so everything follows our wills, our desires. Nature gets very little say. Oddly enough, though, Christmas cannot wait, does not wait, nor can it be rushed or suddenly called up just because we feel like it. But why?

Given that we are so profoundly enslaved to convenience, it is remarkable that we have not moved Christmas to a time of year when travel would be easier and safer or when a burst of spending would be more helpful to the economy. But the fact we haven't done so yet—even though almost no one believes Jesus Christ was born on December 25—suggests our attachment to Christmas is strong enough to resist the temptations of sloth and laziness, which means that even if we doubt the traditional date of Christ's birth, we don't doubt that something uncanny takes place during the season we celebrate His birth.

A conventional view of time and space can account for our curious refusal of Christmas to be liquidated and splashed broadly across the calendar. The belief that there is a right time for some things—not just an opportune time, an expeditious time, but a genuinely *proper* time—implies that time is not merely objective and strategic, but that moral and aesthetic concerns are bound up with time, as well. If time is not merely objective, there must be something outside of time from which time derives its potency. When we object to eggnog in July, we do so because time itself is measured not only by seconds, minutes, and days, but by Goodness, which is not bound by time but makes time possible. Our reasons for objecting to eggnog in July are thus intuitively metaphysical, even though they strike us as simple common sense.

During the Christmas season, heaven and earth draw close together. Stars descend from their fixed realm and lead men from place to place. Signs of God are no longer communicated to common men through prophets, but common men receive signs directly from God. For the shepherds, the Messiah was laid in a manger, a feedbox. For the astrologers, the Messiah was revealed in the zodiac. For Joseph, who shared a name in common with the most famous dreamer of the Old Testament, the Messiah was revealed in a dream. For the Virgin, the Messiah was revealed through miraculous conception. For humanity, the Messiah came as a human. Everyone who learned of the Messiah received a sign after his or her kind. In *On the Incarnation*, St. Athanasius suggests the Second Person of the Trinity might have come as "sun or moon or sky or earth or fire or water," but came in our form so it would be easier for us to understand Him. The signs of Christmas are personal and intimate, unlike so many of the signs of Yahweh in the Old Testament. W.H. Auden once said the first Christmas took place in "the stable where for once in our lives / Everything became a You and nothing was an It," and such poetry makes sense of the Gospel writers' depiction of Christmas as a world in flux, a world where subject and object have returned to their conjoined state, just as they existed in Paradise, just as they were before Eve's materialism. But how could Christmas not be Paradise? Paradise was not simply a lush garden, but the place where God walked with man "in the cool of the day," for it was His presence that made Eden paradisiacal. On Christmas, the knowledge of God began seeping out of every created thing once more, His presence was incarnate in man, and the angels, who from time immemorial had only ever sung to God in worship, sang also to man.

We put off the enjoyment of Christmas things until the Christmas season because we are not alone in the cosmos, and the guests with whom we long to enjoy Christmas are not only human, but divine, and come to Earth only at the time heaven appoints—just as the angel descended at God's decree to stir up the healing pool of Siloam.

In the meantime, we cannot conjure them. But we can wait.

In Defense of Santa Claus

The very center of modern debates about Christmas is the date of Jesus Christ's birth, although Santa Claus sits just outside the center. In the United States, Santa Claus is the most readily identifiable icon of Christmas there is. He is probably more widely associated with Christmas than Christ Himself, which is one of the reasons so many Christians are skeptical of him. Santa's rise to prominence over the last hundred years strikes many Christians as a move calculated to diminish the role of Christ. Of course, the belief that Christ now holds a diminished role in the celebration of Christmas also relies upon a confidence that, many centuries ago, Christians celebrated Christmas with an austere and contemplative piety. Such confidence must be supported with faith or naïvete, for there are no facts to back it up. Christmas has been a rather raucous affair for many centuries—so raucous, in fact, that the first people who ever attempted to ban Christmas were not secularists, not atheists, but prudish Christians. Suffice to say, Santa Claus is not some late secularist intrusion into an otherwise prim, solemn holiday.

The debate among Christians over Santa Claus is older than social media, which means I can recall it from my youth. As a child, my parents told me there was no Santa Claus and so I regarded with suspicion and incredulity those families who would "*do* Santa," that odd and awful little turn of phrase. At the age of eight or nine, I could not possibly imagine why parents would tell their children Santa existed and so I judged them arbitrary, cruel, and malicious. My parents were also uncertain why anyone would tell their children Santa existed; however, I grew up in the 1980s and my parents were deeply attached to evangelical fashions, which meant I was trained from a very young age to fear strangers and avoid anything that referenced magic. My mother's suspicion of magic ran so deep, I can remember her throwing up her hands in desperation when Oreo briefly adopted the slogan "Unlock the magic." Even sandwich cookies were going over to the dark side. My parents' fear of magic probably informed their distrust of Santa, whose whole operation is funded by magic reindeer, a magic sled, a magic bag of toys, elves, and a potentially blasphemous omniscient awareness of our sins. Nonetheless, I was encouraged to be polite and not spoil Santa Claus for all those benighted children out there who "raved in the incurable madness of impiety," as St. Augustine once put it.

My parents' fear of magic was part of "the Satanic panic," a widespread cultural phenomenon of the 1970s and 1980s which saw evangelical Christians become distrustful of anything with dark spiritual undertones, including Dungeons & Dragons, the Smurfs, Cabbage Patch kids, heavy metal music, the celebration of Halloween, and references to the occult in films and popular music. The Satanic panic almost completely failed to transfer from one generation to the next, though, for very few people who married in the ten years following the World Trade Center attacks have raised their children to fear and loathe magic. A good deal of Christianity's present comfort with magic has to do with the release of Harry Potter books and films, as well as the *Lord of the Rings* franchise, and rising interest in *The Chronicles of Narnia*, all of which explicitly deal with magic, and all of which do an admirable job instructing readers and viewers to virtue. Now nearly at the age of forty, I have absolutely no friends who object to Harry Potter on the grounds the series exonerates witchcraft. Oddly enough, none of us inherited our parents' fear of the occult.

I should add, though, that while the Satanic panic had its origin in evangelical Christianity, plenty of other denominations and traditions were comfortable borrowing evangelical fears. The Satanic panic cut across the Protestant mainline and extended well beyond it. However, having lost our fear of magic (and the devil), Santa Claus holds an odd, uncertain place in the Christian imagination and so we have returned to our various tribes for instruction on what to do with him. When I refer to our "tribes," I suppose I mean our churches, although I am really referring to our social media enclaves, which is where our truest and deepest beliefs are furnished.

Allow me to briefly enumerate the major positions on the matter of Santa Claus:

> **The pietist** is opposed to Santa Claus because he is neither described in the Bible nor scientifically verifiable. The pietist

regards Santa Claus as "a lie," and not a noble one. Adults who tell children there is a Santa Claus are not simply playing a game. Rather, they are short-sighted dolts whose children will someday discover that Dad is Santa and then become suspect of everything their parents have ever said. What is more, the pietist believes Santa Claus was invented to sell products, make money, secularize Christmas, and distract from the celebration of Christ's birth. Pietists also tend to be fond of reminding fellow Christians that "the Bible never says we must celebrate Christmas," and frequently complain that the Christmas season is entirely too long.

The hard Nicholist also believes that Santa distracts from God, and yet the hard Nicholist regards Santa not as an ersatz Christ, but an ersatz St. Nicholas. The hard Nicholist snorts when he sees Santa, rolls his eyes at the mention of Santa in Christmas songs, and is always ready to deliver a sermon or history lesson on the subject. The hard

Nicholist considers himself "pretty well read" and is either Catholic, Orthodox, or a very opinionated Presbyterian. He is almost always a man.

The soft Nicholist also finds Santa much inferior to St. Nicholas but does not think Santa a threat to St. Nicholas or to Jesus. The soft Nicholist is not so much disgusted by Santa as he is baffled that anyone would prefer him to the miracle-working, Arius-slapping bishop of Myra.

The pragmatist thinks St. Nicholas a Catholic superstition but finds Santa Claus a helpful psychopomp who, regardless of being fake, nonetheless inspires children to real obedience during the month of December. As the haggard father of real children, the pragmatist is glad the legend of Santa exists; however, apart from the material comfort the legend brings, the pragmatist has no affection for him.

The sentimentalist loves the myth of Santa Claus for the same reason he loves

A Christmas Carol and *It's a Wonderful Life*. While Santa Claus is "not factual," it would be nice if he was. What is more, Santa represents something good and is thus allowable for the same reason Plato's "noble lie" was allowable.

The common man does not know why people argue about Santa Claus but finds him an unobjectionable and aesthetically pleasing part of the month of December.

And, finally, **the mad metaphysician** is a fully-grown adult (with a car, an ulcer, and a bank account) who believes that Santa Claus is, in fact, *actually* real.

With the exception of the pietist, I am more or less content that any of these positions is allowable, though I think some better than others. I myself am a soft Nicholist, which is to say I love St. Nicholas very much, and I think Santa Claus a needlessly colorless myth in comparison. In other words, why drink Seagram's when you could have Hendrick's? Were it not for St. Nicholas, though, I would probably enjoy Santa Claus far more than I do. Christmas produces its share of mediocrity and kitsch and Santa

Claus is a significant part of that schlock—nonetheless, Santa Claus is a far more handsome and pleasing myth than he needs to be. He is from the old world and vexed rationalists often compare him with God, both facts which incline me to favor him.

The revival of interest in liturgy among Protestants over the last twenty years has led many to convert to Orthodoxy, Catholicism, and Anglicanism, and recent converts soon discover all three traditions not only credit the miracles traditionally associated with St. Nicholas but set aside one day every year for his remembrance. The stories attached to St. Nicholas of Myra's legend are often the new convert's first encounter with hagiography, which makes the new convert all the more zealous to tell friends about him. Every December, social media accounts now fill with links to stories and articles about St. Nicholas and so knowledge of Santa Claus' rival is now increasingly common among the laity of many American denominations. Renewed interest in St. Nicholas has proven to be a mixed bag for Santa Claus, though. On the one hand, Santa Claus and St. Nicholas have a few significant traits in common, which means those who venerate St. Nicholas might be apt to look kindly on anyone who imitates him. On the other hand, St. Nicholas of Myra is far more powerful than Santa Claus, accomplished more amazing feats than Santa Claus, and has the added benefit of being real.

If there is a case to be made for Santa, he should be defended as he is widely known, not according to some esoteric history that virtually no one has ever heard. In the age of the internet, scores of pundits claim to have the real inside story on Santa Claus (and the real inside story on Christopher Columbus, Pocahontas, and pretty much every other widely known or celebrated figure). Some people claim the real inside story is that Santa Claus is a department store creation. Others claim he is an anglicized version of some pagan Swiss legend. Others think Santa a good bit like the Super Bowl, a syncretistic melting pot of economics, entertainment, religion, and fanaticism. Regardless of his origin, Santa ought to be attacked or defended for what he now is: a rotund, red-clad old man with a white beard who lives at the North Pole and annually pilots a reindeer-drawn sleigh filled with toys made by elves for children. He enters our homes by way of the chimney, eats milk and cookies we leave out for him, and fastidiously keeps a list of which children have and have not behaved themselves. He rewards the righteous and very mildly chastises the wicked.

Is this a good story?

It is an *okay* story. It could be better, but it could also be far worse.

Above all, it is a *common* story. Santa Claus is one of several dozen mischievous, whimsical figures from folk stories across the globe, all of which tend to run together after you have heard a few. A handful of elements are common to all. The Santa-like figures dress in a regal fashion. While rarely stated explicitly, they are immortal. They usually appear towards the end of the calendar year. They are the exclusive benefactors of children, but they arrive with a hint of danger, as well. The fact that Santa figures are not simply American, not simply Catholic, and not simply Western (the Russians have Ded Moroz, a dead ringer for Santa) means a reasonable man will not dismiss them out of hand. Anything so old and so universally beloved of Christians deserves a hearing.

Of course, very few Christians who dislike Santa dislike him as such. It is not the fact that he wears a red suit, or drives a reindeer sleigh, or comes down the chimney that anyone finds objectionable. Rather, Christians object to parents who tell their children that a fictional person like Santa Claus deserves real love or fear. Lying does not become allowable, it is argued, merely because the lie is a cute one. What is more, if children are conned into good behavior on false pretenses, what sort of behavior should we expect when the pretenses are revealed for what they truly are?

To such objections, allow me to put forward a single competing claim: the idea that it is "a lie" to tell children that Santa brings their gifts is preposterous.

Santa is pretend, as are all his ilk. For this reason, Santa is for children. Children pretend, adults do not. What is more, reasonable adults pretend *with* their children and on *behalf* of their children. When a little child walks into the kitchen and says, "Meow. I am a cat! I want some milk!" only a bona fide atheist would respond, "That is a lie, Suzie, and St. John teaches that murderers, sorcerers, adulterers, *and liars* will go to the second death in a lake which burns with fire and sulfur." I say this despite the fact Suzie is not a cat and despite the fact that liars do, according to the Beloved Apostle, go to their second death in a lake of fire. And yet, when a reasonable parent hears that Suzie the cat wants some milk, the reasonable parent responds, "Here is some milk, little cat."

Children claim to be all manner of things: turtles, ninjas, cowboys, kangaroos, crayons, and good parents simply play along. A little child who claims to be a tiger is no more a liar than an LSU sophomore who claims to be a Tiger, and Santa Claus is somewhere between the child-tiger and the LSU Tiger. Santa Claus is both the mascot of Christmas and a child's fantasy, albeit a fantasy created and sustained by adults; however, few parents sit their children down and tell them about Santa. Children hear about Santa on the streets (or from the bulk bins near the entrance of Target) and inquire of their parents what he is. So, too, only a few children must be told Santa is not real but figure it out around the time they quit claiming to be cats that want some milk.

The sort of dream logic play that children naturally, intuitively begin around the age of five or six—wherein little human beings claim to be animals, fictional characters, even inanimate objects—is an early manifestation of the kind of poetic logic at work in Scripture whereby rocks are Christ, servants are kings, wine is blood, and death is life eternal. The smoky, heady realm in which servants are kings (and God is Man—the Man) is hard for rationalists and materialists to endure. One must become a little child again in order to endure such a place. There is little hope for adults who had the inclination to fantasy ripped from their heads while still young.

I suppose the revelation that "Santa isn't real" comes as a shock to some children; however, by itself, this is not sufficient evidence to prove *all* children must be disabused of the Santa myth the split second they hear about him on television or radio. Some children keep pretending to be tigers until they are quite old, then they are distressed to hear their parents forbid them from playing tigers. Such a child might protest, "But you told me I was a tiger when I was six," though such complaints are both unlikely and unreasonable (even for children).

Nonetheless, if a child cries when he finds Santa is pretend, this strikes me as an entirely fair response. As fond of maturity as I am, a good deal of growing up is pure misery. Some of the misery of growing up involves learning certain things are real which we could not possibly have imagined as children, like the Third Reich or abortion, while other miseries involve learning things are not real which we thought a given, like Santa, of course, but also the free lunch and easy friendships. When we speak of Santa Claus, we must remember we are speaking of a thing that appeals to children, and children are the kind of human beings who walk up to one another and ask, "Would you like to be my friend?" and then form genuine bonds of affection which may last for years. Their thoughts are not our thoughts, neither are their ways our ways.

In *Oedipus the King*, Sophocles teaches that man is half-beast, half-god, for like the beasts, man dies, but like the gods, man contemplates his past and future. The nature of man is tragic, though, because only man contemplates his own death. The animals do not contemplate their deaths because they do not contemplate. The gods do not contemplate their deaths because they do not die. But man is stuck in the middle. And yet, perhaps children are the truest icons of humanity, for they also bear similarities to beasts and gods, albeit not as Sophocles suggested. Like beasts, children do not yet contemplate the future; but like angels, children are innocent. I say this as someone who has two children, as someone who has seen the pettiness and anger of children, the tantrums, the hitting, and theft and so forth. *If* little children sin, they do not sin like adults. Little children simply have not been given custody of their own personhood, a fact which is testified to by their complete lack of shame. Like the unfallen Adam and Eve, children walk around the world naked and confident. Their cries of pain and outrage are not moderated whatsoever by a knowledge of others. The only other human beings with such honesty and abandon are those who have momentarily forgotten themselves at learning a loved one has died. Childhood as such ends when a child becomes capable of bearing children, which happens around eleven or twelve, which is also the age many Christians also describe as "the age of accountability." At puberty, children become self-aware just as Adam and Eve became self-aware after they sinned. And just as Adam and Eve wanted to dress themselves, around the age of puberty, children want to dress themselves, too. They become embarrassed of the clothes their parents give them, for those clothes make them feel naked and exposed. Entering adolescence, children hide from their parents, just as Adam and Eve hid from God after they sinned. Like Adam and Eve, adolescents cannot be disciplined through corporal punishment, but must be cut off from their privileges lest they hurt themselves irreparably. The numerous analogs between the newly fallen Adam and adolescent psychology suggest that whatever comes before adolescence is a kind of prologue or precursor to full-fledged reality, not reality itself. I have met obedient six-year-olds, but I have never met a *wise* six-year-old. So far as little children go, real virtue is as rare as real vice; however, not all children are the same, for some make very fine company and others are awful. So much of childhood is preparation for the moment God turns custody of our souls over to us and our actions have lasting, eternal consequences.

When a child cries upon finding Santa was never real, it is not really Santa they are crying over, but the end of a certain naïve passage of youth. While the claim might seem tinged with the mock-heroic, the child of seven or eight who has just learned the truth about Santa Claus is just a bit like the newlywed who discovers what life is like two months beyond the honeymoon. There is a sense in which a honeymoon is real, but given that honeymooners are usually flush with cash, have no real work to do, eat all their meals out, and make love twice a day, there is also a sense in which a honeymoon is not real because it is not sustainable. But it is uncouth to disabuse little children of the existence of Santa Claus for the same reason it is boorish to brag to honeymooners and newlyweds about "how much more difficult things get." For God's sake, let them enjoy the fantasy while it lasts.

So, Santa is alright, pretending he brings presents is alright, and crying when he no longer brings presents is alright, too. Children are far more shocked to find out sex is real than they are to find out Santa is not, though a reasonable parent might delay both talks for the sake of a child's innocence. The fact of the matter is that little children cannot always handle the whole truth, do not need the whole truth—and for a brief period of time, benefit more from fantasy than from the brutal, unvarnished, no-spin-zone facts.

All the same, I never told my children that Santa Claus

was real. Rather, I have told them that St. Nicholas is real and that he brings them presents on December 6th, which is his feast day. So far as St. Nicholas goes, though, I might actually be a mad metaphysician, for there is some part of me which believes St. Nicholas does in fact bring them gifts each year, even though I myself pay for the presents and leave those presents in their shoes by the door after they go to sleep.

My contention that St. Nicholas brings my children gifts is born of the fact that Scripture describes charity as a unifying power so deep and so mysterious, it sometimes blurs the horizon of autonomy which separates one person from another. In St. Mark's Gospel, Christ guarantees unlosable rewards for those who give as little as a cup of water "in My name." When Christ prophesies the Judgement in Matthew 25, He tells his followers that the charity they give to the hungry, the naked, and the imprisoned is mystically rendered unto God Himself. Christ does not merely approve of charity, He somehow shows up to receive charity in person. So, too, the man who gives his life to God "no longer lives," but Christ lives in that man. Charity is not a rational power, not a scientific power. Selfless love is that power by which the cosmos was created. To this day, a glorious, uncanny, and often unnerving ambience attends acts of charity. The only thing in the world more overwhelming and more unexplainable than great tragedy is great generosity.

The tradition of giving presents to children on the feast of St. Nicholas derives from the saint's most well- known "miracle," his secret gift of gold under cover of night to a desperate man whose sudden poverty had tempted him to sell his three daughters into slavery. The anonymity of St. Nicholas's gift is remembered today in the "secret arrival" of presents for children overnight. Of course, were it not for St. Nicholas, I would not give gifts on his feast day. The gifts are "from St. Nicholas" in the sense that I want to be like St. Nicholas, and in *imitating* him I *become* him, just as Gabriel told Zechariah his son would "go . . . in the spirit of Elijah," and Christ later declared John the Baptist to be Elijah himself (Matt 11:14). Every act of imitation is an act of becoming.

What is more, both Santa Claus and St. Nicholas are winking ways out of taking credit for gifts. In the Sermon on the Mount, Christ cautions His followers to not perform their works of charity in public, lest they receive the reward for their generosity now. If they are willing to wait until later to be repaid, God Himself will repay, and Christ promises us that God repays much better than human beings do.

We teach children to secretly perform their good works whenever we credit our own good works to those whose witness has prompted our actions.

God has stacked the deck in favor of love, which means the rules which govern charity are wonderfully unreasonable and magnificently unfair. Religious and nonreligious people alike intuitively understand the strangeness of love. We give to the poor, but we also give to the poor *on behalf of others*, which is an odd thing to do when you think about it. From time to time, my students purchase gifts for Oxfam in my name then give me Christmas cards informing me of the fact. Perhaps you have received such notices before: "Five goats have been donated to a small village in South Africa on your behalf…" For lack of a better term, I believe such gifts *count*. I don't believe they are fake. I don't believe it is a naïve fantasy to do good works, declare them the works of another, and hope God will reward that other person accordingly. However, I believe the one who performs good works on another's behalf receives credit for those acts, as well, and that God has set up such outrageously slanted, unfair incentive programs because He loves charity that much. Philanthropists sometimes communicate the dazzling unfairness of love by matching, doubling, or tripling any donation made to this or that charitable organization during a particular timeframe: "For every dollar you give, I will give three dollars." That's not just love. That's beatific vision logic. That's wishful thinking incarnate. We have learned such thinking from God Himself.

God is love and love is wild, uneven, and unimaginably wide open. Is Christianity not grounded on the hope that the good works of another can be mystically received by we ourselves? Is that not outrageously unfair, and yet unfair to our advantage? Or is the imputed righteousness of Christ nothing more than a weird outlier, an unrepeatable anomaly, and not a blueprint for all reality?

While I prefer St. Nicholas, the sight of Santa Claus reminds me of the small, fanciful people who yet innocently believe in him, and so Santa Claus is a gentle call to simplify my wants, give up my awful adult vices, and trust in God once more with a child's simplicity of heart. It is good Santa exists.

When to Start Listening to Christmas Music

While debates about Christmas music never quite reach the fever pitch of arguments about the dates and origin of Christmas, after listening for just a minute, one quickly senses both sides are holding back quite a lot for the sake of shame. Over the last several years, two distinct arguments have arisen over Christmas music: the first concerns the propriety of listening to secular Christmas music, and the other concerns the proper date to begin listening to Christmas music.

I should begin by saying the contentious question

of when to begin listening to Christmas music is a red herring. The real question is, "Why listen to Christmas music at all?" Once we have sorted out this question, we will know when to hit play on "Silent Night," at very least, and perhaps "Feliz Navidad," as well.

So far as I can tell, there are four schools of thought as regards the timeliness of Christmas music, and they are as follows:

> First, the **rigorist**. The rigorist believes that Christmas music should not be enjoyed until Christmas Day actually comes. The pleasures of Christmas must be ascetically deferred so that the holiday does not become a hedonistic foothold for the devil. The rigorist opines, "Listening to Christmas music before Christmas is like opening presents before Christmas. Wait. Learn a little self-restraint. The pleasures of Christmas music will be waiting for you when the 25th finally comes, and besides, you won't be sick of the tunes by then."

Second, the **decemberist**. The decemberist does not believe a fellow must wait until the 25th to listen to Christmas music, but he is a bit disgusted at the secular world's itchiness to begin the shopping season. While not as ascetic as the rigorist, the decemberist also wants to stave off the early indulgence which leads to Christmas burnout. He thus pleas, "Can we *at least* wait until December to begin listening to Christmas music?" and he cannot imagine finding the question unreasonable.

Third, the **commoner**. The commoner does not have an opinion on when Christmas music should begin playing. He does not think the matter rises to the realm of "should" or "should not," but is content that society at large will determine when is the right time to begin hearing "All I Want for Christmas Is You" in Kohl's. The commoner regards the return of

Christmas music to the mall much like Laura Ingalls Wilder must have regarded the return of prairie flowers in early spring, sometimes a week earlier and sometimes a week later, but always as nature knew best.

Fourth, the **psychopath.** Much like the rigorist, the psychopath believes the time for Christmas music is definitive and inviolable, but he believes *that* time is *all* the time. Even in July or on Valentine's Day.

Although I am a decemberist, I will confess an equal amount of sympathy for each of these positions. Over the next ten years, I might easily slide into any of the other three. This might strike you as quite relativistic, but so far as I know, no denomination or church tradition places requirements on members to wait (or not wait) until a certain day of the year to begin listening to "Jingle Bells" or "I Saw Three Ships," which means the decision is entirely based on what the individual can bear (and not based on their mere wants, though more on that later).

As an Orthodox Christian, I believe the liturgical celebration of Christmas is obligatory and that keeping the Nativity fast and the Advent feast are duties, as is attendance at Nativity and Advent services. The sacred constitution of Christmas *is* Christmas proper—so while a man is *free* to celebrate Christmas by watching *It's a Wonderful Life* and setting up a tree, he *must* celebrate Christmas in the manner prescribed by God through His church. Nonetheless, Christians err greatly when they treat secular traditions and manifestations of Christmas as detractions from Christmas proper. There is nothing wrong with "Silver Bells." In fact, there is something very, very right about it—something which is a little more right with every passing year.

For some, "Christmas music" brings to mind Brenda Lee and Nat King Cole. For others, the Choir of King's College Cambridge. While the latter is vastly superior to the former, secular Christmas music should not be disparaged simply for being secular—especially not pop Christmas tunes from the 1940s and 1950s. Songs like "White Christmas" and "Silver Bells" induce a particularly rich and heady nostalgia in Americans that helps them become little children again and Christmas is a holiday oriented around childhood, the Christ child in particular. The older "Silver Bells" gets, the younger the spirit it conjures.

When I say Christmas is oriented around childhood, I do not mean Christmas is some sort of universal holiday that does not require Christian faith to celebrate truly. Christmas is nothing other than the celebration of the Second Person of the Trinity taking on flesh that all flesh might take on divinity, thus making it the most Christian of Christian holidays and not liable to secularization. And yet, one would have to be blind to not recognize the distinct appeal of Christmas to children.

While the feast day of St. Nicholas is weeks away from the Nativity of Christ, the two events have been logically, naturally, and providentially conflated, for children are unique beneficiaries of St. Nicholas's most well-known and oft-retold miracles. Children play with toys year-round, yet toy drives are particular to late November and December. The celebration of Christmas is driven more by children than by their parents, for children are far more loyal to Christmas traditions than adults. Children have a profound ability to remember "what we did last year." There is even something about the sight of the *infant* Christ which softens the hearts of the most recalcitrant iconoclasts, who willingly yield to the crèche in December, even though the sight of the crucified *adult* Christ in April brings great consternation.

While Christ came as man to save man, children are even more attached to the fact He came as a child. Unlike adults, children are not afraid of Jesus. They like Him. Adults have a hard time taking the infancy of Christ seriously because they know He ultimately turns into the Man Who says, "If your right eye causes you to sin, pluck it out," but children accept the infancy of Christ with simplicity of heart.

When we speak of "the Christmas spirit," we simply mean a spirit of generosity and open-handedness. While the earth mysteriously, invisibly inclines toward generosity during Advent, it is mankind's responsibility to act on such inclinations and to *augment* them, as well. Christmas music reestablishes within our souls the pathos of Christ's selflessness, but also His innocence, the innocence of children, and our own need to become little children again that we might faithfully bear witness to Christ. It is quite hard to be generous and selfless, though. We need all the help we can get. So, inasmuch as "Silver Bells" or "I Saw Three Ships" move a man to works of faith and charity, July is a fine time to listen to such music. While music *reminds* us, music is not merely a mnemonic device that brings old truths to mind. Music is an animating spirit; thus "I Saw Three Ships" is not a shopping list of virtues, but a spell. If such songs do not prompt a man to works of faith and charity, not even Christmas Day is an appropriate time to listen to them.

Of course, the same is true of all Christmas traditions, not simply Christmas music. The tree, the spices, the fake holly and ivy, the cards, the red and green, the silver and gold, the lights, and the wrapped gifts are not simply seasonal aesthetic preferences, nor are they mere reminders. Rather, these traditions provide real help in establishing (for us weaklings) the mystical reality of Advent and Nativity. They are not superfluous to the formal liturgical celebration of Christ's birth, but emerge from the bounteous, gratuitous holiness which pours out of the church calendar and splashes on a host of nearby secular things. The tree, the spices, the red and green are secular references to the sacred, which means they are not quite sacred, but not merely secular either. The tree and spices and even "Silver Bells" are the holy secular, which is not a distraction from the holy, but evidence of just how generous holiness is. The sacred cup overflows, as the psalmist says, and everything near the cup is charmed.

Put another way, while "Silver Bells," candy canes, and Christmas trees are not holy, they nonetheless emerge organically from what is holy. They are secular tributes to holiness, cultural labors which aim to refashion what is earthly after what is heavenly. Rather than dismissing secular Christian traditions as mere consumer preferences, we should recognize them as part of our calling to bring a higher, better world down to earth— and to live in a manner worthy of that world. If we will not live and move and have our being in that sublime, generous, and open-handed world, neither do we deserve the décor.

In Defense of George Bailey

Any debate about the merit of *It's a Wonderful Life* is, by this point, largely superfluous. There is no cinematic equivalent of Homer, but no film comes as close as Capra's 1946 Christmas classic. Seventy-four years is a long time for a pop culture artifact to last. Consider for a moment that the best-selling book of 1946 was Frederic Wakeman's *The Hucksters*, a title which has never been reprinted. First editions of that gem currently sell on Amazon for about a dollar. Hitchcock's *Notorious* was also released in 1946, and while that film still plays well, it doesn't show at hundreds of theaters across the globe every December.

Yet, despite the universal acclaim Capra's film has garnered, come December, the naysayers have their naysay. There are three kinds of *Wonderful* detractors. The first kind claim the film is cheesy, the second kind claim the film is theologically or philosophically dubious, and the third kind are zeitgeisty grinches who whine that anything more than ten minutes old is racist and chauvinistic. So far as I am concerned, the third kind can sit on a tack, and the first kind tend to be garden-variety dads who also complain Christmas is overly commercial. It is the second kind of naysayer I worry about.

I should clarify, though: I do not so much worry about the second kind of naysayer as I do about the naysayer's wife and kids and Twitter followers. As a defender of every traditional and quasi-traditional Christmas thing known to man, my concern is that philosophical or theological attacks on the film will needlessly complicate the common man's confidence in its goodness. History grinches and culture grinches already want the common man to feel a little guilty about celebrating Christmas, for this is the real intent behind all those badly researched articles that declare Christ was not really born on the 25th or that Christmas was originally Saturnalia. In similar fashion, the common man cannot refrain from tears at the generous conclusion of *It's A Wonderful Life*, though I fear those tears might trickle to a halt on subsequent viewings if theological arguments against the film are taken too seriously. Unlike bad cash-grab *Grinch* remakes or the terrifyingly vapid *Love Actually*, *It's A Wonderful Life* is not a guilty pleasure, but a pure one.

The theological objections to *It's A Wonderful Life* range from the petty, by which I refer to the depiction of God and His angels as casually chatty points of light, to the more predictably Lutheran protestation that the final half hour of the film aims to prove that George Bailey was not an abject sinner, but a good man whose good works earned God's favor. To be frank, I don't think the first objection worth dealing with. It's the second objection which has some real teeth.

Having seen the film a dozen times since I was a kid, I simply cannot accept the claim that the hero is presented as some kind of faultless human being. If there is a faultless human being in the film, it's George's wife. The Lord loves a cheerful giver, but He'll take a reluctant one like George Bailey. George's plans to make a name for himself are foiled year after year, and George does not take this in stride, but his frustration mounts until he begins lashing out at his friends, his family, and himself. Shortly before George goes out to kill himself, he shouts at his children and Mary, his wife, asks, "Why must you torture the children?" The question is not phrased in such a way as to suggest George's angry behavior is uncharacteristic, but that it has been this way for a while. Thus, Clarence the angel does not come down to prove to George that he is a good person, just that his good works have been seen by his Father in heaven. His good works have not saved him, for Clarence comes at the behest of George's family and friends, who pray with earnest supplication that God will "watch over" George and "help him."

Some viewers object that Clarence's work merely plays to George's hubris, and that as opposed to George coming to God, George merely comes to himself in the end. However, the idea that George has not already come to God is usually extracted from a single line in his suicidal prayer wherein he claims he is "not a praying man." This is a curious claim, though, given that he is twice described in the film as going to church to "weep and pray" on momentous days of World War II. His wife prays, his kids pray, and George prays occasionally. Less some awful *Fireproof*-esque "come to Jesus moment," George Bailey is a lifelong Christian who simply doesn't go to church very often.

As for the criticism that Clarence comes to flatter George, it must be noted that Clarence doesn't so much show George the world without him, but the world as it would have been had George gone off and pursued all his vainglorious plans of fame and fortune. Clarence does not come to tell George he should count his blessings and then name all the pleasant things still at play in his life, like his pretty wife and his house and his decent health. As

Boethius shows in *The Consolation of Philosophy*, counting your blessings is a fine thing to do when the chips are up, but when the chips are down, counting your blessings is a distraction from the more dire need to make your petitions known to God. If a man counts his blessings in the midst of his trouble, he might *forget* his trouble and forget to beg God to arise and scatter His enemies. If you would not pertly respond, "Count your blessings," to Christ on the cross after He bellowed the cry of dereliction, then do not tell others on their crosses to count their blessings. Be the blessing. "Count your blessings" is just a pious veneer to put on "Physician, heal thyself."

Instead, Clarence insists that George should be grateful for all the good things God has done *through him*. At the film's denouement, Clarence says "You see, George, you really *had* a wonderful life." The word "had" is key, for after recounting the good things George has done, Clarence does not declare George a "wonderful man." In performing his wonderful deeds, George has *received* the wonder of God. When Clarence returns George's life to him, it is with the tacit charge that he not become weary in doing good. The cash which slowly piles up before George and Mary in the closing moments of the film is not money they can spend on their own pleasure, but money they will put back into the lives of their friends. Every dollar placed before George in the last five minutes of the film is money he will give away over the following weeks. There is simply nothing about the close of the film which does not point to a working man joyfully returning to his work.

If Clarence's experiment with George seems impious, it is Christ Himself Who first opens up the question of whether the world is better off with all the people who presently occupy it. As for Judas, Christ declares that "it would have been *better* for that man if he had not been born." If this claim does not challenge the sovereignty of God, then neither does Clarence's assertion that the world would have been *worse* had George never been born. Having seen the world without George Bailey (or, rather, the world without George staying in his home town to grind out his salvation with fear and trembling), we are left with the embarrassing question of what the world would be like without Potter (way, way better), and the introspective question of what the world would be like without ourselves. Clarence sets the bar high, though, and does not justify George's existence merely on the grounds that his kids are cute.

When the credits roll, the viewer is not so much proud of his own life as he is grateful that people like George Bailey exist. The viewers feels the weight which Clarence has placed on George to be virtuous, and to "use worldly wealth to make friends, so that when it is gone, you will be welcomed into an eternal home." Out of Christ's strangest parable comes cinema's most enduring film.

Meditations on the Creche

Act 1 The Family Holiday

Part I. One may not say that Christmas is a child's holiday (as I have done in this book) without simultaneously saying it is a family holiday. Images of the family dominate Christmas. Fireworks are the icon of July Fourth. Champagne is the icon of New Year's Eve. The grill is the icon of Memorial Day. However, the ultimate icon of Christmas is the creche, which depicts the holy family gathered around the Christ child. Christmas is really the *only* holiday in America—Christian or otherwise—which centers on the family, for either Mary or St. Joseph or

Christ Himself is absent from depictions of Pentecost, the Annunciation, the Transfiguration, and all the rest. So far as celebrations go, the fully-grown hedonist may take July Fourth, New Year's Eve, Memorial Day, his own birthday, Friday nights, Saturday nights, Summer (in general), and the whole of his twenties as an excuse for reckless self-indulgence, but mothers and fathers must seek out some higher, better kind of pleasure on December 25.

These higher, better pleasures of Christmas always set the merely sensual pleasures we ferret out the rest of the year in high contrast, for every mother and father who puts any effort at all into the celebration of Christmas is reminded just how much real satisfaction and joy can be derived from blessing a child. When we make New Year's resolutions a week after Christmas, we do so with the lingering knowledge that no sensual pleasure, morally allowable or otherwise, has ever made us as happy as happy children make us. Our resolutions reflect this, and our resolutions last as long as we remember it.

The celebration of Christmas is not merely an earthly

phenomenon but a cosmic event which encompasses all people and all of nature. At the same time, Christmas is apt to teach mothers and fathers many hard lessons, lessons which are extraordinarily hard-won for bachelors, and the chief of those hard lessons has to do with economies of happiness within a marriage.

Before he marries, a man is free to seek out happiness on whatever terms he chooses. He may do so sinfully, righteously, or in a way which is not sinful but neither brings him much spiritual fruit. There are scores of activities, hobbies, and pastimes which may be "lawful" for a fellow, but which are "not helpful," as St. Paul distinguishes in 1 Corinthians 6:12. For instance, a man may love baseball, vintage running shoes, motorcycles, or mid-century modern furniture, and the pursuit of these hobbies may bring him happiness and satisfaction. It may be that when work gets hectic and his leisure time is put on hold for several months, he often thinks, "I would be happier if I had an afternoon to work on my motorcycle," yet his work has taken him away from the things that make him happy and so his life is simply less satisfying.

After he marries, though, a man spends the next decade of his life learning that the old exchange rate for happiness, whereby he traded his time for things which intrigued and delighted him, no longer works in quite the same way. The common American proverb, "Happy wife, happy life," is not a burden placed on wives to be happy, but a man's acknowledgement that attempts to seek out private happiness to the exclusion of his wife cannot make him happy for long. This is not to say a man must give up all his hobbies after he marries, but it does mean that, in marrying, he solemnly agrees to never be much happier than his wife.

Some bachelors have hobbies that can be easily adapted to family life. However, if an unmarried man has hobbies and pastimes that are expensive, involve numerous trips away from home, or many hours spent in front of a computer, he will find after marrying that his private pleasures are tainted with regret, for his hobbies will take him from his family (which will tempt his wife to bitterness), or his family will take him from his hobbies (which will tempt the man to bitterness). He may attempt to incorporate the lives of his wife and children into his hobbies, but he should be ready for his wife and children to try to incorporate him into their hobbies, as well, which will mean he has fewer hours for his own pleasures, or that his family (a bunch of novices and rookies) are always slowing him down. He may nonetheless persist in his hobby with his novice wife and rookie children, but he should be ready to not get the same personal happiness from his hobby that he got while a bachelor—at least, not for quite some time.

On the one hand, then, marriage implies a great loss of control, for a man no longer directs his efforts at happiness toward himself. On the other hand, it is far easier to make someone else happy than it is to make yourself happy. The man who buys himself a cup of coffee may enjoy the coffee, but he enjoys it on a purely material, sensual level. However, were his wife to bring him the same cup of coffee—though he never asked for it—he would enjoy it both on a sensual level and a spiritual level, for he would regard it as a gift.

Every gift-giver imbues his gift with a soul—his own—for gifts are born of personal sacrifice, even if the sacrifice is small. If men did not have souls, gift-giving would simply be a slow form of suicide. For this reason, we are hesitant to throw away gifts, even unwanted ones, for they are icons and sacraments of the people who gave the gifts. Men keep dogs they do not like for years for just the same reason.

It may be argued that coffee is a gift even if the man buys it for himself, for the coffee is indirectly the gift of God, Who causes it to rain in Costa Rica, and while the man paid for the coffee himself, it was God Who knit the man together in his mother's womb and gave him the power and strength to earn his money. However, these observations are far more consistent with an ascetic, contemplative way of life, and while Christians in work-a-day lives occasionally acknowledge this truth, mustering up *the same* heartfelt gratitude for the coffee a man buys himself that he feels for the coffee his wife brings him is well-nigh impossible. It is far easier to *acknowledge* that all things are a gift of God than it is to feel *genuine thanks* for them. But when other human beings give us gifts, they participate in the generosity of God and make it easy for us to give thanks to Him not only for the gifts, but for the people who give them. It is easier to love men than to love God, a fact which St. John addresses when he writes that "anyone who does not love his brother, whom he has seen, cannot love God, whom he has not seen" (1 John 4:20). Simply put, it is very difficult to give thanks to God on our own, but other people can make the generosity of God visible and obvious. In this, gift-giving allows us to participate in the salvation of others, and thus work out our own salvation at the same time.

While a man does not need to be married in order to understand the economies of divine love, marriage profoundly limits the total number of pathways a man may take to happiness. Many of the short, harmless paths to pleasure before marriage simply dead-end after marriage. At the same time, many paths to pleasure which are difficult to tread before marriage become far easier after marriage. As a bachelor, I often lived in squalor because I did not like to clean. As a married man, I find it much easier to clean and tidy because it pleases my wife. As a bachelor, cleaning my apartment afforded me some pleasure, but not nearly as much pleasure as watching television. As a married man, there is simply more pleasure to be had from a happy wife than from an hour of watching television, even on rare occasions when there is something good on. If I am watching television when my wife walks in the door, there is a good chance she will casually, benignly ask what I am doing. The frustration I feel at having to say, "Nothing," or, "Just watching television," cancels out whatever pleasure I had in watching television. On the other hand, I greatly enjoy the greeting, "You vacuumed." Marriage is a mystical union, but a happy marriage often necessitates both husband and wife behaving like hoteliers and restaurateurs who want repeat business.

So far as economies of happiness go, what is true for husbands and wives is all the more true for parents and children. In the same way that there is more happiness to be enjoyed in blessing your spouse than in blessing yourself, there is more happiness to be enjoyed in blessing your children than in blessing anyone else. The joy of children is not simply a gift to the family, but a functional contribution, for unhappy children make for unhappy parents, as well. Happy marriages do not simply run on happy spouses, but on happy children. Unhappy children not only cause a marriage to sink, they are the effect of an already sinking marriage. There is no greater gift children can give their parents than to be happy, and there is no greater gift parents can give their children than a reason to be happy, and thus the health of the family is entirely synergistic.

All gifts are synergistic, though, because all gifts are repaid with the joy of human communion. Gifts tear down walls between people. Every genuine gift reveals the gift-giver's knowledge of the one receiving the gift, which means that walls between people are torn down when gifts are exchanged whether we want those walls torn down or not. In the same way, good works are not transactional but synergistic, for good works involve the expenditure of earthly resources and are repaid in communion with God.

When Christ was born, he was showered with gifts from the magi not because of what He had *done*, but because of what He *was*, and to this day, Christmas still makes children highly conspicuous. Every other holiday celebrates the *accomplishments* of great men, but Christmas is a celebration concerned with the mere *arrival* of a little child. Children are beautiful because they are useless, especially little children. Like a Caravaggio painting or a Beethoven symphony or St. Peter's Basilica, children offer nothing *materially* valuable to their parents. We all need food, clothing, and shelter to survive, and thus money and coats and homes are useful, even necessary. And yet, children are not necessary for the survival of their parents. From a purely material standpoint, Caravaggio makes our lives more difficult, for stewarding the beauty he has bequeathed us is costly, and the money we spend creating and sustaining beautiful things could be spent instead on things that keep hearts beating. On the other hand, Caravaggio and Beethoven make life good. Beautiful things "seem to promise a reconciliation beyond the contradictions of the moment, one that perhaps places time's tragedies within a broader perspective of harmony and meaning,"[1] and so beauty gives meaning to all the suffering we undergo to secure food, clothing, and shelter for our families. The sheer gratuity of giving gold to a little child is a token of the infinite generosity which sustains all being. Giving gifts to children is a pious act of faith.

Christmas is a great boon to children not only because they enjoy getting gifts, but because of all people, children are the easiest to justify forgetting. We forget the elderly because we rarely see them. We forget the poor because we judge them lazy or vicious or because numerous government agencies already exist to remember them for us. Our own children can be hidden in plain sight, though. Children are surprisingly resilient and can float for weeks on mediocre food and terrible entertainment. They are cheaply pacified, and years may pass before our slapdash, thoughtless treatment of them becomes obvious.

---

[1] Hart, *The Beauty of the Infinite*, 16.

They are easily deceived and easily forgive. Yet, the creche makes the helplessness of children an unavoidable point of contemplation every time we see it. The fact that Christ was once a helpless child means we cannot excuse our neglect of God by saying, "He can help Himself." Newborns look alike and sound alike, which means that no human being bears a closer physical resemblance to Christ than an infant. It is never easier (or more natural) to "discern the Lord's body" than when holding an infant during the Christmas season. The helplessness of children reminds us of the helplessness of Christ, Who prophesies in Matthew 25 that He will someday receive every act of charity as though performed unto Himself.

The helplessness of children means they are bereft of all the avenues adults usually take to distract themselves from boredom and misery. Children have no money. They cannot get drunk. They cannot go where they want, when they want. When they cannot sleep, they may not lay awake on the sofa, flipping through channels until they get tired. They cannot call their friends when they feel helpless. While it is a sin to spoil children, it should also be noted that if a little boy wants something, unless someone gets him that thing, he will simply never have it. The complete dependence of children is a call for mothers and fathers to take up the burden of Christmas, which means curtailing their private pursuits of pleasure and arranging a celebration of Christ's birth for their children where the giving and receiving gifts seems *fitting*.

Purchasing gifts for children at Christmas is a social obligation every parent is ashamed to forgo, but beneath the knowledge one ought to *buy* something for his children, Christmas similarly prompts mothers and fathers to want to *do* something for their children. Every father knows the disappointment of giving his children gifts which they neither want nor appreciate. While it is easier to make a child happy than an adult, there is a wrong way to give a gift.

Part II. For the first several years after they were born, my wife and I heaped up gifts for my children on birthdays and Christmas. They spent an hour opening the gifts, then they were irritable and cried for the rest of the day. This happened not just once, but often enough that I slowly came to dread the opening of gifts. It was not until my third or fourth reading of *The Consolation of Philosophy* that I understood why opening twenty wrapped packages in a row made my children miserable. The problem was not simply that my children were being given too much on December 25, but that they weren't being given enough for the eleven days after Christmas.

As a little child, I unreservedly loved Christmas, but about the time I entered high school, I often found myself depressed around the end of the year. Christmas break means far more free time than usual and winters in the Northwest (where I lived) were typically harsh and bleak, which meant I usually spent the latter half of Christmas break indoors, where there was little to inhibit endless self-reflection. A little seasonal melancholy is not inappropriate, nor is it necessarily destructive. When a man lays down to sleep at night, he is entirely alone with his thoughts, for conjuring sleep depends on complete inactivity. Nothing remains to distract a man from his failures, his hopes, and his worries whilst he waits for sleep to come, and so many men make vows to God to live better while on the cusp of oblivion. That time between Christmas and the return to school is, for many students, like a prolonged laying down to rest. These eight or ten days are the most leisurely in the whole calendar because during this time, there is far less work to distract a fellow from the ennui, boredom, discontent, and disenchantment which bubble below the surface of his soul the other fifty weeks of the year. The melancholy which sets in after Christmas may be nothing more than a troubled conscience coming to terms with itself. Inasmuch as Christmas melancholy leads to repentance, it is a gift.

At the same time, because Christmas is a holiday oriented toward little children, teenagers often find Christmas disorienting, for they are no longer little children, but neither are they responsible for little children. Two weeks off from school means teenagers must spend more time than usual around their parents; however, at about the age of fourteen or fifteen, many teenagers no longer view their parents as a means of getting what they want, but as obstacles which keep them from the things they most want, like boyfriends and autonomy. Unlike summer, most teenagers do not get jobs just for Christmas break, and very few teachers assign any homework. Sports are often on hiatus, as well. Thus, Christmas has a tendency to constantly remind teenagers of their curious, unglamorous place within the life of the family.

My own Christmas melancholy carried on into college because I understood that Christmas wanted me to be generous, but I had almost no money, no one depended on me for anything, and so I lived in a stupor of self-interest and self-fulfillment. For many years, I sadly reflected every December that I was nearly immune to the inclinations toward sacrifice and joy which others felt. When Christmas Day finally arrived, I had nothing but recollections of how I used to love Christmas. Remembering how I used to love Christmas also reminded me that I used to be good, or at least much better than I had become, for I knew that after

I reached the age of twelve, every year of my life was more filled with sin than the year before.

While I cannot give a universal account of the after-Christmas blues, I know that what arises in the human heart at the end of the year is not merely a desire to *feel* better but a need to *live* better. A man's melancholy on December 26 is a measurement of just how little he received on the 25th, and how little he received on the 25th is a measure of how little he gave before the 25th. Christmas was a profound offer to mankind from God when Christ was born in Bethlehem two thousand years ago, and Christmas is a profound offer from God today, but accepting the offer requires preparation, which is a thought that worries the kind of American Christians who fear Catholicism and like to pretend works righteousness is an actual temptation we face.

By the time my eldest child was four, my wife and I had begun putting a plan together which would make the giving and receiving of gifts on December 25 a fitting thing to do. Looking back years later, I could not help but notice a connection between my old Christmas blues and the foul mood that possessed my children after opening a heap of presents. Simply put, an unqualified glut of pleasure rots the soul. It is easy for adults to recognize this in children, and yet adults are often reticent to conclude the same is true for themselves, because it means admitting there is something in life which is more important than seeking pleasure—and that this more important thing might involve suffering.

The more gifts you stack up in front of a child, the less each gift means. The moment a child finishes opening the first of twenty gifts, he cannot help wondering if there are better gifts in the remaining nineteen packages. Adults scroll endlessly through Netflix menus for the same reason. The possibility always exists that there is something even more suited to our preferences on the next screen, thus we begin to evaluate every option for all the ways it fails to perfectly satisfy every last desire we have. The more options we consider, the pickier we become. The average American now spends over a hundred hours every year just looking at Netflix menus. Likewise, the child who knows there are twenty more gifts to open only sees the gift in his hands for its insufficiencies. The more gifts he opens, the more particular his desires become, which leads him to find each gift he opens less appealing than the one before it. When beginning to scroll through Netflix menus, an adult lingers over the plot description of new titles, but after twenty minutes of looking, he blows through one screen after another without even seriously considering any of the titles as a real possibility. So, too, a child with twenty gifts to open moves through the heap with increasing rapidity. The first might take a minute to open, a minute to consider. By the tenth gift, the paper is torn off voraciously and the object inside instantly assessed and set aside.

The solution, really, is to only give a child one gift on Christmas Day.

Act II: Looking Forward to Christmas

When I was younger, it was not so much the *preparation for Christmas* which began the day after Thanksgiving as it was the *celebration of Christmas*. Precious little distinguished the 3rd of December from the 25th, for it was all one long train of fudge and sugar cookies from the moment the leftover stuffing was gone. By the time the 25th rolled around, I was merely doing more of the same. Presents rolled in early, a variety of different parties dotted the calendar from the first week of December through the last. The 25th was confusing because nothing in particular really *arrived* on that day. Nothing new began. Everything was simply carrying on as before. The same music, the same parties, the same rich food. The 25th came and nothing changed. Presents were opened, and then everyone was supposed to feel... what? Far happier than the day before? But why? It is unreasonable to demand that a man begin acting much happier when you have given him nothing to be happy about. Properly preparing our hearts for Christmas means giving ourselves spiritual and material reasons for being happier on the 25th than on the 24th.

If the common man's Christmas now revolves too much around opening gifts, it is because opening gifts on the 25th is the last remaining vestige of asceticism which attends the celebration of Christ's birth. Modern men who are willing to wait for absolutely nothing else still wait until the 25th to open gifts. We indulge in all manner of festal food and jolly gatherings throughout December but waiting to open gifts is a monk-like practice that attends Christmas even for those who turn up their noses at all other forms of worldly renunciation. However, if a man opposes fasting of all other kinds, why fast from opening presents? If it is more joyous to wait for gifts, why not wait for prime rib and Époisses de Bourgogne, as well? During Advent, renouncing sensual pleasure is a kind of holy pageant wherein the remarkable Christian history of waiting is publicly performed on a massive scale. Asceticism is a drama, even if it is performed with no more talent and poise than that of a ten-year-old boy dressed in shabby bathrobes for a Christmas play.

Giving up fancy food and parties during Advent means something substantial changes on the 25th. The weakness of the human heart is acknowledged in fasting, for the pleasure which comes from breaking the fast helps create the spiritual joy of the holy day. A man with profound spiritual discipline could simply command his soul to suddenly grieve deeply at the thought of Christ's crucifixion, or to suddenly become joyous at the thought of Christ's birth, but people with such discipline are exceedingly rare and do not read books like this one. It is hard to be suddenly happy, but it is easy to be suddenly happy for the wine, cheese, and roast beef one has not tasted in a month. Going from a state of not-opening-gifts to a state of opening-gifts is simply not significant enough to warrant a change of heart, so while waiting to open gifts relies upon the logic of asceticism, it simply does not produce many of the spiritual benefits of asceticism. On the other hand, eating and drinking are a constant human preoccupation. When we wake in the morning, we think of food, prepare food, eat food, then wash the dishes. We drink coffee on the way to work, get more coffee after arriving at work, then begin thinking about lunch an hour later. At lunch, we heat our food, eat our food, wash our dishes, stow our dishes, and less than an hour later, we are getting more coffee and, in the back of our minds, beginning to mull over dinner. On the way home from work, we stop by the grocery store, contemplate the foods we want, put those foods in our carts, pay for our food, drive our food home, take our food in, put our food away, then take it out once more to cut it up, season it, and cook it. Then we set the table, move our food from the kitchen to the dining room, eat our food, clear the table, wash the dishes, and put the dishes away. An hour later, we begin to think of dessert.

All this to say, the man who undertakes an ascetic diet is *significantly* altering his life on an hour-by-hour basis.

The oldest, strictest Christian traditions commend fasting from meat, dairy, and alcohol during Advent. Since becoming Orthodox twelve years ago, I have been required to live according to such dietary restrictions during Advent, although my adherence to these requirements has varied. Some years, I keep the fast carefully. Other years, I don't. Having seen it from both sides, I can say that giving myself an edible reason to look forward to Christmas forty days out makes the celebration of Christmas far sweeter.

Some might say that looking forward to Christmas because of fine wine and roast beef is no less shallow than looking forward to Christmas because of wrapped boxes. But if this is true, why look forward to Christmas at all? A certain kind of modern Christian is apt to reply, "We should look forward to Christmas because it was the day Christ was born, not because of presents and fine wine." However, what does it mean to look forward to Christmas? How does one do it? How does one look forward to Christmas while making the bed on Thursday, December 14th, at 7:13 a.m.? The idea that we should look forward to the day Christ was born but not to wrapped gifts and fine wine depends on a belief that wrapped gifts and fine wine are an arbitrary way of celebrating Christ's birth and that we have chosen such forms of celebration for selfish reasons. When this argument is directed at those who refuse any kind of renunciation at all during Advent, it obviously carries some moral weight.

However, wrapped gifts and fine wine at Christmas are not arbitrary, and neither are candy canes and decorated trees. These traditions are born out of an older way of viewing time and being. Nonetheless, many modern Christians are functioning materialists and atheists who believe the Christian religion is nothing more than an ornate constellation of books, prayers, and ideas whose primary purpose is that of a mnemonic device that helps people remember. Remembering is thought an exclusively intellectual act that takes place entirely within the realm of conscious, easily explainable thought. Anything beyond articulated thought or communicable speech is basically useless. Every tradition associated with Christmas exists to help us remember Christ's birth, and the greatest use of recalling Christ's birth is right moral action.

But the older view of Christmas (in fact, the view which produced the Christmas holiday itself) was less concerned with remembering than *becoming*. Within this view, the liturgical and social traditions of Christmas allow us to enter more deeply into the life of Christ, which is to say that decorating the tree is something of a mystical activity.

This idea tends to be very offensive to the sort of

Christian who is obsessed with remembering because it defies the idea that one's salvation is nothing more than a sudden, divine, judicial decision in favor of the one getting saved, in which case the Christian religion is really nothing more than a club for like-minded people who enjoy remembering the same things, most of which occurred over the span of a few years in Palestine back in the first century AD. The church is entirely auxiliary to salvation, though, and has, over the centuries, constructed a rather elaborate façade of traditions and ceremonies which cover over the embarrassing fact that it is ultimately unnecessary and really only exists at the behest of its voting, tithing constituents. The older view, however, takes the church as playing an ongoing, necessary role in salvation and affirms that an individual's salvation begins at a fixed moment, but deepens and matures over the course of a life. This maturation is not thought to be a superfluous "sanctification," but the *very point* of salvation.

All this may seem a needlessly contentious theological diatribe in the midst of what might have been a rather tame reflection on making the most of Christmas; however, the confusion and depression which settles into many Christian hearts the week after December 25th is often the result of a profound encounter with just how hollow, extraneous, and *optional* modern religion truly is. The man who fails to spiritually prepare for Christmas in turn receives very little on Christmas, which both confuses and saddens him. And yet failing to spiritually prepare is usually due to theological convictions that preparation is pointless because there is nothing really to prepare for. One does not need to prepare *to remember*. Remembering and preparing to remember are one and the same task. Thus, the Christian who thinks his religion is primarily concerned with remembering spends the entire month of December celebrating Christmas, then the actual holiday comes and goes, the man enjoys no spiritual revelation, and a day later he begins to wonder whether his religion has any point. This is by no means an overreaction, because if his church cannot stage a profound encounter between parishioners and God on Christmas—a season of year when the church has more clout, more beautiful traditions, and more cultural inertia than at any other time—can his church ever stage such an encounter?

Very few churches still hold services on Christmas Day, which means the average Christian is led by his church to the very cusp of the holiday and then liturgically abandoned the morning of the 25th. Having been a member of more than a dozen different Christian denominations before I turned thirty, I can say the typical reason most churches give for not offering services on Christmas Day is that "people prefer to stay at home with their families on Christmas morning," which is a banal explanation that also accounts for why so few self-professed Christians go to church on the average Sunday. Many families feel the painful absence of worship on Christmas morning and attempt to fill it by reading the story of Christ's birth from St. Luke's Gospel before opening presents or eating breakfast. While such families clearly have their hearts in the right place, it takes all of two minutes to read the story of Christ's birth, the story is typically read while everyone is yet unbathed and still dressed in pajamas, and no one needs even to stand. Having sat through such quasi-ceremonial readings when I was younger and having briefly instituted them in my own home during the first several years of my marriage, I can honestly say they did more harm than good. Had every pretense of religiosity been set aside the morning of the 25th and the whole family simply plowed into the gift wrapping and Irish cream with wild, hedonistic abandon, I might have more easily set aside my fear that something was missing—because something would have *obviously* been missing, there would have been no doubt or ambiguity over the matter. But the easy, hasty nod to religiosity on Christmas morning was neither hot nor cold, neither hospitable nor hostile. It acknowledged that the sacred *ought* to be part of the 25th without actually granting a sacred experience. Thus, I often reflected on the two-minute reading of Luke 2:1–20 over the remainder of Christmas Day and wondered, "Was that really enough? Was that necessary? What did that actually accomplish? Why did we do that?" In the midst of such questions, it struck me as uncomfortably, yet unavoidably true that church attendance was pious for many reasons, not the least of which was that going to church was a bona fide hassle. The fact that no one was willing to go through with this hassle to corporately sing and adore God on Christ's birthday struck me as rather pathetic, and this feeling of having cheated God—or, at least, come up with a purely specious reason for not troubling myself—permeated my reflections on Christmas for days to come.

The renunciation of fine things during Advent is not merely an aid in remembering the five thousand years mankind waited for the Messiah to come, but rather a way of *entering* into the anxiety which plagued the Earth between the Fall and the Nativity, as well as the hope which grew out of this anxiety. Every act of imitation is an act of becoming. Unlike the ancient Jews, we live in the time of Christ; however, both modern Christians and ancient Jews alike have been asked by God to wait. The Jews waited for the arrival of the Messiah, but Christians wait for His return. Giving up rich foods is not simply a way of remembering that we are waiting. It is the waiting itself, the hoping itself. When we celebrate the arrival of Christ on Christmas, we also look forward to His return and to the end of this age. Hope is an active virtue, a painful triumph over despair. Hope is not simply whatever pleasant distraction takes the place of the thing we are waiting for.

Giving up fine things during the prologue to Christmas is only half the equation, though, and the other half involves celebrating all twelve days of Christmas, as has been a Christian tradition for many centuries. In both the East and the West, the Christmas season runs from December 25th through January 6th, which is the feast of Theophany (the baptism of Christ) in the East and the feast of Epiphany (the visitation of the magi) in the West.

With the revival of fortune which #liturgy has enjoyed over the last fifteen years, more American Christians are celebrating the twelve days of Christmas now than when I was a child; however, committing twelve full days to the celebration of Christmas requires patience and preparation, and unless some kind of fasting has been suffered in the days leading up to the 25th, the family will be burned out on Christmas before the three French hens arrive. Asceticism makes room in the heart and the stomach for the feast which comes after. Christmas ought to be an extended celebration, but it is naïve to think that a hearty, genuine celebration can begin on the 25th if the celebration has already been running for a month.

Several years ago, my wife and I began making a concerted effort to keep all twelve days of Christmas, and so we limited the children (and ourselves) to opening just one gift a day. This not only provided some of the fodder for a twelve-day celebration, it also gave the children time and space to truly enjoy each gift they were given. Twelve days of celebration does not mean twelve days of continuous, uninterrupted sensual pleasure, which I think both unenjoyable and unsustainable. Rather, the 25th kicks off a spate of celebrations, but each day between Nativity and January 6th need only contain one special activity, like a trip to the theater, a game, a visit to some little spot out of town.

My wife and I have also made a habit of giving our children experiences as opposed to things. Because my children do not eat lavish foods during Advent, and because they only open one gift on Christmas Day, their primary interest when looking forward to the 25th is not a toy or gadget they have asked for, but the festal meal we share, which is to say they look forward to something the family does together, not to some object they will retreat to their rooms and enjoy. Several days before Christmas, my wife and I wake early and take the children out shopping for all the food we will eat on Christmas Day and for several days after. When the time comes, the children are involved in preparing the food, as well. A five-year-old is not too young to sloppily pour milk and glop butter into a pot of boiled potatoes for mashing. As early as possible, Christmas should be a thing children do, not a thing merely done to them. While the gift of cheap, disposable toys is not entirely out of the question, I find it depressing to give gifts for Christmas which will be forgotten by the following Christmas. To not remember what was given just *last year* because it was either broken or abandoned by March certainly dampens any excitement at going out to buy gifts *this year*. The same is true for husbands and wives, who ought to make it a goal to give one gift every few years which the other person will keep until they die. The best way to make a Christmas full is to fill it with past Christmases.

Another great benefit of fasting during Advent and then feasting for all twelve days of Christmas is that the holiday has a genuine beginning and ending. When I was a teenager, the indeterminate nature of the Christmas season made the whole affair seem arbitrary and tawdry. If we continue celebrating Christmas after the 25th, why? At what point is Christmas genuinely over? After a full month of Christmas parties and fudge, attending one more party on December 29th seemed to me a desperate, gluttonous attempt to keep the party going, even though everyone was already quite done with it, perhaps in the same way teenage boys at a slumber party like to stay up as late as possible, even though no one really enjoys it after three in the morning.

If Christmas does not have a real beginning, then neither does it have a real ending, and we simply quit celebrating when we are sick of it, which means that Christmas is just one more thing that caters to our desires and which we feel free to discard whenever we feel like doing something else. On the other hand, if a robust Advent fast is undertaken, followed by twelve days of feasting, one recognizes a right time to take down the tree as opposed to taking it down simply because everyone has begun to feel guilty and fat whenever they look at it.

While the celebration of Christmas has slowly created hundreds of widely recognized cultural traditions, many families also have private traditions they observe throughout December, which may include ceremonially decorating the tree, the preparation of certain foods on Christmas Eve, and so forth. From time to time, I ask my students about the private traditions of their families. Many respond exuberantly, but between one-third and one-half of them tell me their families don't have any Christmas traditions. The first time I heard a student claim his family had "no personal Christmas traditions" I did not believe it, but this occurred early in my career, and having had more than a decade to teach classical literature and contemplate where traditions come from and how they develop, I no longer find it hard to believe. I can recall several occasions from my childhood when my family did something related to Christmas during the month of December—from cutting down our own tree, to baking cookies—and before the task was even finished, someone said, "We should make this a tradition. We should do this every year," and there was always something in my heart which sunk at hearing these words, for I knew it wouldn't happen. I knew that no one would remember it the following year. Modern people tend to believe that traditions are pleasant things we do for their own sake or for the sake of remembering something important, but such a belief about tradition is born of the nominalist philosophical conviction that meaning itself is arbitrary and that meaning can be gained or lost or changed simply because we feel like it. When discussing the durability of certain traditions, I sometimes ask my students to propose a tradition which could be implemented in their own families this year and still be observed by their great-great- grandchildren a hundred years from now. Unsurprisingly, most of them simply take some activity they already enjoy (travel, shopping) and propose doing that activity on a certain day every year, although they often glumly tell me when turning in their work, "I don't think this is going to work." They are correct, of course, but I later tell them that the assignment was entirely unfair and that creating a tradition from scratch that will be followed a century later is impossible. Most traditions which last for centuries either preserve human life, redeem some ancient suffering (by symbolically recreating it in a safer environment), or celebrate a great triumph over suffering. However, people do not suddenly, voluntarily undertake life-threatening peril or profound pain, which means that the kind of traditions which last for generations cannot be conjured or created. They must be discovered. My more sagacious students usually propose family traditions that piggyback on well-established cultural traditions.

For the Christian mother and father who want to develop Christmas traditions for their family (and not do the holiday differently every year), there will be a distinctly modern temptation to reinvent the wheel, to start from scratch, or to begin scouring the internet for Pinterest pages and blog articles about "fun and meaningful Christmas activities and traditions for the whole family." However, a consumerist approach to religiosity—whereby we shop for purpose, evaluating a range of possible rites and ceremonies for their attractiveness while also considering their respective price tags—typically involves isolating the three or four most enjoyable aspects of more venerable traditions, removing everything difficult or esoteric about them (usually because it is "outdated," "superstitious," or "no longer relevant"), and ultimately leaving people with nothing more than a hollow reference to something real. Traditions that are chosen and edited in such a manner are not actually traditions, though; they are fashions, for there can be no doubt that the most traditional forms of

Christianity are better social media fodder than modern forms of Christianity, and that the dressing and hardware of Orthodoxy, Catholicism, and Anglicanism are far more Instagramable than, say, Methodist or Baptist Christianity, which sadly explains quite a bit of their popularity over the last fifteen years. However, undertaking a simple, ascetic diet during Advent resists the Modern impulse to put a pious gloss on the pursuit of a hip, recherché online persona that prompts flattering questions from friends. An ascetic Advent diet also stands to become an actual tradition, because it will not be abandoned for something more pleasant, as it was never pleasant to begin with; neither will one become bored with such a diet, for it was never exciting to begin with. Traditions chosen like products off a supermarket shelf never inspire real obligation or duty; however, fasting through Advent is a disciplinary hassle which defies the modern Christian want to pillage the most aesthetically pleasing elements of other traditions and cobble them together.

Admittedly, during the first several years in which my

wife and I abstained from meat and dairy during Advent, we experimented with odd dishes, ate a lot of foreign cuisine (which is more often vegan than American dishes), dabbled in exotic vegetables and grains, and often commented to one another that fasting from meat had opened up a new culinary world to us. But that kind of enthusiasm wears off rather quickly (it may have been entirely related to the fact that we were in our twenties), and now, like most Orthodox Christians, we spend Advent eating rather dull meals which are prepared quickly and eaten plainly, all the while looking forward to the celebration ahead of us. Early on, we were also both apt to discuss the health benefits of fasting and to regularly note our progress toward fitness as measured by the bathroom scale. Over the course of a decade, though, one slowly comes to terms with the fact that any weight lost during Advent is gained back during Nativity, and that one may even put on weight during a fasting season given that every kind of carbohydrate is both allowable and easy to prepare. Simply put, both the novelty and the material benefits of an ascetic diet wear away rather quickly and one is left with the fact that tasty food is a dependable consolation against the miseries of life and that without it, one must seek consolation elsewhere.

As pained as a prosperous nation is to admit it, the old proverb "Hunger is the best sauce" suggests that desire and delight are integrally connected and that those who are perpetually satiated miss out on flavors that can only be accessed by way of a little starvation. For human beings, hunger is only instinctual in the short run, but when drawn out over time, hunger is experienced in the soul, as well. Animals experience hunger as pain and threat, which means they satiate their hunger as soon as they feel it. Humans are contemplative beings, though, which means we eventually perceive hunger as a loss of love, a loss of communion, and an injustice. The things we look forward to turn over many times in our minds before they finally arrive. Hope is protean. For the chaste young fiancé, *anticipation* of the wedding night transforms the act of making love into a hundred different kinds of experiences. Sometimes it strikes the man as romantic, at other times it seems purely erotic, or even comic, or it takes on theological dimensions and seems like a strange ritual akin to baptism or circumcision. Were the man to meet some woman at a bar and find himself in bed with her an hour later, there would be nothing to anticipate, and so the act would be sub-intellectual. Anticipation gives a man time to see the anticipated thing in all its diversity, in all its various relationships with everything else in the world.

As fun as it is for parents to surprise their children, I have found my children enjoy things far more when they know they are coming. When I tell them that breakfast tomorrow is "going to be a surprise," their curiosity runs wild all evening and what I offer them the following morning does not meet the highest reaches of their fantasy. On the other hand, if I tell them I am going to make them pancakes, they can tell each other many times before the following morning that they "can't wait for pancakes." Anticipation for anything is hunger. The anticipated life is the saucy life, the life adorned by imagination.

When we do not have sufficient time to anticipate

a thing, it is hard to meet that thing (especially a great thing) with the proper degree of thanks. The man who anticipates this or that thing experiences it a thousand times before experiencing it once; thus he knows how and why he should be thankful for it when it comes. In those thousand experiences, he lives inside the event, discovers the corners, is given room to speculate, perhaps even goes through shades of disappointment in the thing before he even truly knows it. The hotly anticipated event is often so idealized that it is most deeply enjoyed when it is over. The event itself passes as a dream, a vision, and becomes an even more profound source of enjoyment and mystery in retrospect.

In the end, the distance between the ascetic and the voluptuary is not all that great. The ascetic does not shun physical pleasure but rather takes a liturgical and sacramental approach to pleasure. The ascetic knows that pleasure stripped of imagination is neither sustainable nor

---

2 Hart, David Bentley. *The Devil and Pierre Gernet: Stories* (Eerdmans, 2012). p. 24.

satisfying. A period of fasting prior to Christmas allows us the space we need to connect physical pleasure with something beyond this world. Within such a framework, pleasure is not a self-terminating end to itself, but a sign of something greater.

What If Christmas Is Exactly What It Purports to Be?

Part I. Every December, Christians are subjected to a host of dour, skeptical, and cynical claims about Christmas. We are told that, long ago, Christmas was actually a pagan holiday. We are told that Jesus was not actually born on December 25th. We are told that Christmas traditions have largely become meaningless, because absolutely no one knows why we eat candy canes, why we decorate trees, or why we wear red and green. But, even if this were not the case—even if Christ was born on December 25th, and even if Christmas was not originally a pagan holiday, and even if we knew why we decorate trees—could anyone possibly deny the fact that Christmas now primarily exist to glorify Mammon?

However, if someone were to compile a list of the greatest unexamined modern platitudes, close to the top one could expect to find "Christmas has become so commercial and materialistic." Long a favorite claim of frowning head-shakers and adults who insist the crust is the healthiest part of the bread, such claims recall some inaccessible golden age when the holiday was pure and undefiled. Evidence for the commercialism of Christmas is omnipresent during December. Consider the dollar bins at the front of Target from late November through New Year's, all the tree-shaped snack cakes, the Santa garbage in every conceivable color of cheap plastic, the Black Friday sales, the bad cash-grab movies with trailers that begin, "This Christmas . . ." and feature bumbling fathers falling from the roof while trying to string up lights.

The idea that Christmas "has become so commercial and materialistic" banks heavily on the rather ludicrous notion that the rest of the year is not thoroughly imbued with such callous qualities, when Christmas is really no more commercial and materialistic than any other time of the year. All year long, Target fills those dollar bins near the entrance with some kind of cut-rate seasonal detritus that, no more than three weeks later, shuffles off this economic coil for the landfill. In our former lives, we were subsistence farmers who made everything for ourselves and many of our children died before being weaned. We traded such lives for lives wherein a church was less than a four-hour walk. We now live in cities, and so we must buy everything. It is not as though we were all going to live in the middle of Manhattan and make our own candles, soap, cheese, shoes, and banjos. How would we find the time? While we can all lament the pandering and cloying quality of the modern advertisement, the fact that, come December, modern corporations put decorated trees and Saint Nick on the same soulless ephemera they hawk the other eleven months of the year hardly means that Christmas has become "so commercial and materialistic."

Christmas has not become materialistic. Materials have become Christmasy.

All things considered the month of December strikes me as the least materialistic time of the year simply because people have a reason to consider their own materialism. Precious little about the Fourth of July gets anybody thinking about the fact that they basically live on bread alone. Further, the same general level of selfishness exists between Thanksgiving and Nativity as exists throughout the rest of the year, though it is undercut by an increased expectation of providing for others. While plenty of people use Black Friday sales to indulge in purchases for themselves, how many people capitalizing on Labor Day weekend furniture sales are giving away sofas? If only one in ten desperate Black Friday shoppers went out for gifts, it would still beat the charitable quotient of every other annual sale combined.

What's more, ours is a culture which accepts the idea of "the Christmas miracle," no matter how kitschy the idea comes across. A surprising number of people are open to the idea that God is more apt to reveal Himself during the Christmas season than at other times of year: everything from visions to sudden expressions of generosity toward strangers counts. If the Christmas season were actually more materialistic and crass than other times of the year, I doubt Advent would inspire such a confidence in the miraculous, for Christ does not do many miracles where there is unbelief. The Salvation Army bell ringers in America take in more than 135 million dollars between November 28th and December 24th, roughly 5 million dollars a day, most of which is collected outside of Walmart stores. Is this the work of a nation that is more materialistic than usual? Does anyone honestly believe the Salvation Army would take in this much if they rang their bells in April? It requires madness or blindness to not recognize that a unique spirit of generosity and open- handedness overtakes Christian men during Advent. There are Christians in this country who *never* give to the poor, and yet during Advent, they are overcome by an unexplainable spirit of liberality and magnanimity which is otherwise absent from their lives. They "give to everyone who begs from you," as Christ commands us in Luke 6, and they give to those who cannot possibly repay. Stories of Christmas generosity from our own era are simply the continuation of ancient traditions which date back well over a thousand years. Christmas seems to have always been attended by lavish giving. Whether historical or fictional, the figures most readily identifiable with Christmas—Ebenezer Scrooge, the tenth-century Bohemian King Wenceslaus, the fourth- century Turkish St. Nicholas, the magi who visited Christ—are all known for their charity.

There are, of course, many ways of rationally explaining all this away. Some might say that people are expected by society to be more generous at Christmas time, and so they only give to keep themselves from embarrassment. Or, they feel guilty for not giving, and their charity is merely to salve a guilty conscience. Or, they enjoy the warm feeling which comes from giving more during December than any other month, and so they do so to put themselves in a more agreeable mood. However, in explaining away Christmas we risk explaining away the whole of Christianity, for the Christmas spirit is simply a microcosm of Christianity. The Christian who dismisses the Christmas spirit as nothing more than a happy pathology must borrow from the same arguments which atheists use to dismiss every work of God in man.

Beside the fact that Christmas draws out greater generosity from more people than anything else does, Christmas is also a time when people who otherwise *never* come to church want to be near God. It is a time when many self-professed atheists, secularists, and agnostics are nonetheless willing to sing hymns praising God. While many Christians disdain people who only come to church "on Christmas and Easter," we ought to rather be grateful that there is one time a year in which those who are closed off to God become mysteriously open to His love. Christmas is a season which softens stony hearts, recalls noble oaths made long ago, and brings to mind not the judgment of God, but His clemency, longsuffering, and mercy. Once a year, the watery zeitgeist parts and we pass through the world a little less soaked by the folly and selfishness which floods our hearts the rest of the time. Christmas is not a game of dress-up which is lucky to have us in a playful mood, and neither is Christmas some tawdry, silly holiday which depends on a sermon to be of real value. Two thousand years ago, Christmas concerned the surprising reconciliation of man and God and nothing has changed about it since then.

What is odd, though, is that none of the evidence presented here in favor of Christmas being *less* commercial than the rest of the year is hidden. Rather, it cries aloud in the streets. The Salvation Army bell ringers, the secularists singing "The First Noel," the toy drives, the bustling soup kitchens, the overstuffed food donation bins, not to mention all the gifts people buy their friends and coworkers . . . all this is common knowledge. Anyone who claims that Christmas is overly commercial is simply not paying attention to the world. Where did the myth of an overly commercial Christmas come from, then?

Part II. I suppose some people will simply not be content unless those who celebrate Christmas do so with a little shame, a little embarrassment over the matter, as though the celebration of Christmas is something we condescend to do, perhaps even against our better judgment. It is permissible to celebrate Christmas, but only if we do so from a critical distance, for Christmas really is a silly child's game which we must dignify with fancy speeches. Such people are genuinely terrified that Christmas is now exactly what it has always purported to be: the timely celebration of Jesus Christ's birth. Given that Christmas is so steeped in tradition, attacking the veracity of Christmas is really a subtle way of attacking everything that is old. Sadly, such attacks are not merely a secularist pastime, for there are a good many Christians who understand that if Jesus Christ was actually born on December 25th, *something* about Catholicism would be vindicated. After all, the December 25 date is nowhere given in Scripture, and if some ancient Christian institution actually had *any* real knowledge of Christ that wasn't contained in Scripture, no matter how small and apparently trivial that knowledge was, that same institution might claim to have other real knowledge of Christ that wasn't in Scripture. Thus, there is a certain strain of Protestantism which has an awful lot riding on Jesus Christ being born on any day *other* than December 25th.

If Christ was born on the 24th or the 26th or "sometime in August or September," then one of the most ancient extrabiblical traditions of the church about Christ is wrong, the singularity of Scripture is confirmed, my access to the truth is really no different than the bishop of Rome's access to the truth, and any other tradition associated with Christmas (or Christianity as a whole) is similarly just an approximation, just a suggestion, and may be endlessly edited to suit our beliefs. At the same time, there are also plenty of Catholic and Orthodox Christians who prefer to view the traditions (liturgical, moral) of their respective churches as nothing more than tools or "resource[s] for our spiritual journeys, not as a mandatory itinerary,"[1] which is less a credo or vice of any particular denomination than an

---

1. Reno, "Fighting the Noonday Devil."

inclination which afflicts nearly everyone living after the Enlightenment.

The fear that the traditional date of Christmas somehow vindicates Catholicism is only furthered when one scratches the history of Christmas and discovers that continental Protestants have a long and dappled history of condemning and even outlawing Christmas. Some Protestant apologists now claim that Presbyterians originally banned Christmas because the holiday was attended by days of heavy drinking and carousing and that the holiday's abolition was simply a public health concern. As someone who believes all the stories about St. Nicholas raising the dead and feeding entire cities with his prayers, I have to say I find this explanation for banning Christmas a bit hard to believe, given that when John Knox banned the celebration of Christmas in Scotland, the day was declared "superstitious." A hundred years later, pious students at the University of Edinburgh burned an effigy of the Pope to mark Christmas.[2] Further, the celebration of Christmas was banned in some early

---

2. "The Scots Demonstration."

New England colonies, with some cities going so far as to hire "mince sniffers" to walk the streets on Christmas Day and smell out anyone baking traditional Christmas foods, which were then confiscated and destroyed. Likewise, certain accounts of Santa Claus's origin also suggest he was simply a less pontifical version of St. Nicholas, who is usually depicted with a bishop's miter and crosier in hand, neither of which Protestants care for.[3] Suffice to say, the so-called war on Christmas is now fought between Christians and secularists, but not so long ago, it was merely fought between Christians. The fact that Protestants have come to accept the celebration of Christmas might mean little in the way of theological changes but might reveal quite a lot about how the lines of society have been redrawn over the last two hundred years. The same denominations which once felt it a moral necessity to *not* wish others, "Merry Christmas," now feel they are boxing their corners by wishing Target cashiers, "Merry Christmas," as opposed

---

3. "The Angels Wanna Wear My Red Suit."

to, "Happy holidays."

However, if modern Protestants are willing to grant that the celebration of Christmas was never really a Catholic superstition, is it possible that admitting the December 25 date for Christ's birth wouldn't really mean selling the farm either?

Of course, some argument in favor of the date would be necessary first. Those who reject the December 25 date are given to saying that "Christ was probably born sometime in August or September," which is not merely an historical claim, but a theological claim, as well, which suggests it does not matter when Christ was born and that God has no interest in His people knowing. Before going further, and as something of an aside, I should note that many debates about Christmas often contain doctrinaire, condescending uses of the word "actually" when the word is by no means justified. Having argued for many years in favor of the December 25 date, I am regularly impressed by the staggering number of people who say, "You know, Jesus wasn't *actually* born on December 25th," as though they have done genuine research into the matter and come to an uncommon opinion, when they have done nothing of the kind. The idea that Jesus was not born on December 25th is now such a routine and customary opinion that virtually no one is capable of making a case for it. Rather, most people justify the claim that Christ was not born on the 25th by saying, "There is just no evidence which suggests He was born on December 25th," which is not only untrue but also manifests a complete ignorance of the matter. Those who claim there is "no evidence" for the traditional date have typically never heard of Hippolytus of Rome or the *Chronograph of 354* or the slew of names and titles one quickly learns when researching the history of Christmas. Such people may as well claim, "There is no evidence the sun is at the center of our solar system," while also admitting they have never heard of Copernicus, Galileo, or telescopes.

If you scratch the surface of the case in favor of the December 25 date, you will find a host of living researchers who are strangely devoted to their cause. The depth of their devotion and the intensity of their fervor must have something to do with the fact that making a case for the traditional date involves a remarkable convergence of academic disciplines: theology, philosophy, mythology, anthropology, history, hermeneutics, astronomy, and apologetics. Just as the Incarnation bridges the divide between supernatural and natural, so the case for the December 25 date brings together highly abstract theories and good old-fashioned historical research.

With that, I should return to the claim that Christ was born "sometime in August or September," and ask whether it makes sense to argue that God does not care if His people know the birthdate of His Son, given everything else we know about Christ's birth. After all, the Gospel writers want us to know who gave birth to Christ (a fact which Scripture declares significant); the circumstances under which she gave birth (a fact which Scripture declares significant); the country where she gave birth; the kind of room in which she gave birth; and the specific manner in which His birth was announced to Joseph (in a dream), to the astrologers (by a star), and to shepherds (in a manger). If all these things were thought significant, why would we assume the day on which He was born was not significant? To this question, a naysayer might respond, "If the date of His birth was significant, that information would have been contained in Scripture," which assumes the only way in which Scripture could indicate Christ's birth would be plainly stating, "And He was born on December 25th." But let us grant that there is a great difference between Scripture "not stating something" and "not stating something *clearly*." It took the church nearly three centuries to sort out the fact that Father, Son, and Holy Spirit were co-eternal and co-essential because the biblical case in favor of these truths is not like, say, the biblical case in favor of Mary giving birth to Jesus.

While it is fair to say that the December 25 date is a Catholic tradition, and Catholics are often accused of being superstitious (both by Protestants and secularists), let us admit that if the story of the star leading the astrologers to Christ were not contained in Scripture, but was merely a tradition of the Catholic Church, there would be no small number of modern Christians who claim the story was invented by the early church out of jealousy for the stories of astrological signs accompanying the births of Roman emperors. Read Suetonius's *The Twelve Caesars* and note how Romans expected their emperors to be born under auspicious signs and on auspicious days. In its relationship to Passover and the solstice, December 25th is just such an auspicious date, the cherry on top of a birth which is richly attended by all manner of other very pagan-esque portents. What is more, if the story of Christ's virgin birth were not contained in Scripture, but was merely a Catholic tradition, the whole world would claim the myth grew out of early Christian hang-ups about the body that are still present in modern Catholic sexual mores.

Before tucking into the evidence in favor of the December 25 date, it is worth asking what kind of evidence modern people are willing to accept. Having lectured many times on the date of Christmas, and having asked my students what kind of evidence they would find persuasive, I know that what most of them want is an ancient hotel registry excavated from Bethlehem with an entry from December 24, AD 0, which reads, "Mary (virgin) and Joseph: Discount stable rate." Anyone holding their breath for such evidence is bound to be disappointed by the actual case in favor of the December 25 date, but the ongoing incredulity of such people is no real loss, because if the case were built on that kind of archaeological evidence, there would be all manner of reports and analyses which concluded the registry was fake (and a dozen other unearthed registries which suggested He was born on other dates), just as there are plenty of reports and analyses of Scripture which conclude it is untrustworthy. In other words, the late antique culture from which the December 25 date emerged required evidence that could not be easily forged or faked, which simply precludes archaeological evidence from playing an important role in any theological matter. This is deeply disconcerting for modern Christians, who believe the New Testament is best understood by experts who have studied Greek, Aramaic, intertestamental history, and first-century Palestinian culture, as though we cannot possibly understand what Christ meant when He said, "You are the salt of the Earth," unless we know the historical role salt played in ancient Roman society. When Christians raised on the grammatical-historical hermeneutic read late antique theologians like St. Augustine or St. Gregory of Nyssa, though, they are often baffled and horrified by what they read, for both theologians approach Scripture as an oracle that can only be understood by those initiated into the mysteries of God.

What's more, late antique theologians rarely treated Scripture as an historical document which emerged at a particular time, buoyed by dated references to the world which could only be understood with a history textbook in the other hand. Scripture was not what the church said long ago, but what God says today, even now, through His church. Thus, St. Augustine teaches that Noah's ark prefigures the church and that the three stories of Noah's ark *might* prefigure Noah's three sons, who repopulated the earth, or the three stories may represent the three theological virtues, or the three harvests of the Gospel (thirty-fold, sixty-fold, one hundred–fold), or the three states of chastity (marriage, widowhood, and virginity). After elucidating all these many possible meanings, others are free to offer *whatever* interpretations of the three stories of Noah's ark they like, provided the interpretations can be "[harmonized] with the rule of faith."[4] A better example of late antique and medieval hermeneutics may be found in St. Gregory of Nyssa's *Life of Moses*, wherein Gregory attempts to interpret the life of Moses as a *moral* pattern by which all Christians should live. He begins by addressing the question of whether women can live like Moses, given that Moses was a man and the wicked Pharaoh wanted all male Hebrew children to be killed. Gregory writes:

> *The narrative is to be understood according to its real intention. For the material and passionate disposition to which human nature is carried when it falls is the female form of life, whose birth is favored by the tyrant. The austerity and*

---

4. Augustine, *The City of God*, XV.26.

> *intensity of virtue is the male birth, which is hostile to the tyrant and suspected of insurrection against his rule. Now, it is certainly required that what is subject to change be in a sense always coming to birth. In mutable nature nothing can be observed which is always the same. Being born, in the sense of constantly experiencing change, does not come about as the result of external initiative, as is the case with the birth of the body, which takes place by chance. Such a birth occurs by choice. We are in some manner our own parents, giving birth to ourselves by our own free choice in accordance with whatever we wish to be, whether male or female, moulding ourselves to the teaching of virtue or vice.[5]*

In other words, every man "gives birth" to strength and weakness, virtue and vice, but the Devil is always trying to cut us off from our strength just as Pharaoh tried to prevent the Hebrews from building an army in the future. This,

---

5. Gregory of Nyssa, *The Life of Moses* (Paulist Press, 1978), p 56.

according to St. Gregory of Nyssa, is the "real intention" of the text.

Many of my students object that this kind of interpretation seems like nothing more than a game, and an arbitrary one at that. The meaning of the text is determined by sheer fancy of the interpreter, who does not seem bound by any discernable rules, and thus the meaning of the text may be endlessly manipulated to suit the reader's needs. Of course, the idea that the mystical modes of interpretation favored by the church for more than a thousand years were "arbitrary" and "changeable" would have struck medieval Christians as quite odd given the inconstant nature of grammatical-historical mode of interpretation. The grammatical- historical method of interpreting Scripture relies heavily on scholarship, and so the grammatical-historical interpreter will have to change his reading of the Bible (which is to say his theology) as often as relevant archaeological data is unearthed. If we assumed a purely grammatical-historical hermeneutic, an entire school of eschatology could be debunked by the discovery of a scrap of first-century poetry or the excavation of a certain Roman vase. If scholarship really is the key to reading the Bible properly, then every dogma depends on evidence to the contrary never being discovered in the future, and every creed and catechism is—like a scientific theory—merely "to the best of our knowledge" and thus subject to endless revision and refinement. Say what you like about St. Gregory's reading of Exodus, it is not beholden to "new studies" and "recent discoveries." For this reason, prior to the rise of the grammatical-historical method of interpretation, theology was a far more stable enterprise than it was after. One could read St. Augustine's *City of God*, which was finished in AD 426, then follow it up with St. Anselm's *Proslogion*, finished in AD 1077, and perceive very little real difference between the two, even though both theologians embraced what strikes modern men as an arbitrary and fickle hermeneutic. On the other hand, twentieth- and twenty-first-century theologians *from the same denomination* often write grammatical-historical interpretations of Scripture just a few years apart which are entirely incompatible with one another. The idea that mystical interpretations of Scripture are less stable than interpretations based on historical data simply does not fit reality, which brings us back to the question at hand.

The belief that Christ was born on December 25th emerged when men like St. Augustine and St. Gregory of Nyssa were the custodians of the Christian intellect. Granted, the December 25 date comes to us much earlier than these two theologians, but they are emblematic of the kind of early Christian tendency to read the Bible as an oracle of God, not an historical document (which demanded historical research to understand). The proof that Christ was born on December 25 would accordingly need to come from some source which could not be falsified or proven a forgery. For this, early Christians looked to the heavens.

But first, a little history. Everyone who honestly sets out to research the pagan origins of Christmas is bound to turn up a number of ironic facts.

Critics of the December 25 date often claim early

Christians chose it for their celebration of Christ's birth because they were jealous of the Roman feast of Saturnalia, which, critics claim, occurred on the same day. In fact, the feast of Saturnalia never touched December 25. It began on December 17 and carried on for different lengths of time but never made it to the solstice. Rather, those arguing against the traditional date of Christmas have confused Saturnalia with Sol Invictus, the feast of the unconquerable sun, which some believe to have occurred on the winter solstice, when the days begin to grow longer. However, historian Steven Hijmans (Roman Art and Archaeology professor at the University of Alberta) argues persuasively in his 2003 paper "Sol Invictus, the Winter Solstice, and the Origins of Christmas" that "there is no firm evidence that the feast of Sol on December 25 antedates the feast of Christmas at all. The traditional feast days of Sol . . . were August 8, August 9, August 28, and December 11."[6]

The emperor Aurelian set apart December 25th for a

---

6. Hijmans, "Sol Invictus," 384-385.

celebration of Sol Invictus, but he did not do so until AD 274, nearly seventy-five years after the earliest Christian claims that Christ was born on the 25th. In several different works (*Commentary on Daniel*, the *Canon*, and the *Chronicon*), Hippolytus of Rome (AD 170– 235) of Rome declared December 25th the date of Christ's birth.[7] Shortly after Hippolytus, Julius Africanus claimed December 25th as the date of Christ's birth in his work *Chronographiae* (AD 221), as well. While contemporary Christians are often told that Christmas was originally a pagan holiday, historical research suggests the very opposite is true and that Aurelian's hijacking of the December 25th date was likely an attempt to subvert well-established Christian claims.

Others arguing against the traditional date of Christmas point to the *Chronograph of 354*, a compilation of calendars made in AD 354 for a wealthy Roman Christian. The *Chronograph* marks December 25th as "Natalis Invicti," the "Birth of the Unconquered," which Christmas critics

---

7. Schmidt, "Calculating December 25."

immediately conflate with the feast of Sol Invictus, a feast for "the unconquerable sun." This is problematic for numerous reasons, not the least of which is that Aurelian's co-opting of the December 25 date was part of a cultural program to establish the cult of Sol in Rome, though the Romans had never practiced solar religions and Aurelian's work had entirely failed by the time of Constantine.[8] Simply put, Roman pagans never took Sol all that seriously, which makes it ludicrous to think Christians would feel the need to wage a cultural campaign against Sol later.[9]

Attempts to marry the "Natalis Invicti" mentioned in the *Chronograph of 354* with Sol Invictus are also suspect because Natalis Invicti is not the name of a holiday mentioned prior to the *Chronograph of 354*, a document created more than forty years after the legalization of Christianity and during a time when Christianity was an increasingly common and even fashionable religion. Given all this, "Natalis Invicti" is more likely a euphemism for

---

8. Hijmans, "Sol Invictus," 387–88.
9. Ibid.

the birth of Christ than a reference to Sol. Besides, by AD 354, Christianity had long established the sun as an icon of Jesus Christ, who was viewed as the fulfillment of Malachi's prophesy that a "sun of righteousness will rise with healing in its wings" (Mal 4:2).[10] In the second century, Tertullian dealt with accusations that Christians worshipped the sun because they faced east to pray and because Sunday was their weekly day of worship.[11] While Christians did not worship the sun, they nonetheless acknowledged that what transpired in the heavens symbolized higher truths, for Moses clearly states in Genesis 1:14:

> *And God said, "Let there be lights in the expanse of the heavens to separate the day from the night. And let them be for signs and for seasons, and for days and years."*

The idea that there should be heavenly and astral signs of Christ's birth is not pagan but comports rather obviously with scriptural accounts of why God created the "lights

---

10. Grout, "Sol Invictus and Christmas."

11. Ibid.

in the expanse of the heavens" in the first place. Besides, Scripture openly declares there were astral signs of Christ's coming. The December 25 date is derived primarily from its relation to March 25th, the day which both Julius Africanus and Hippolytus calculated to be not only the first day of creation, but also the date of Christ's conception and the date on which Christ was crucified. For the first several centuries of Christian history, the age and date of creation was calculated through various methods, like adding together the ages of patriarchs listed in the book of Genesis, but also through extrabiblical histories and by calculating the date of Passover in the past. Through the convergence of all these methods, Hippolytus (and others) determined the world was 5502 years old when Christ was born, that the first day of creation was March 25th, and that when the moon was created four days later, it was "a Passover moon."[12] Hippolytus (and others like him) did not believe the first Passover took place on just any old day of

---

12. Schmidt, "Calculating December 25," 558.

the year, or under *whatever* phase of the moon happened to have occurred when night fell on the tenth plague. Rather, they believed the *particular phase of the moon* on the night of Passover and the *event of Passover* itself were integrally tied. Passover had, to some degree, been typified in the heavens for many thousands of years before the actual event transpired in Egypt. Because Passover is always determined by the phases of the moon, the date of Passover could be calculated retroactively, which is to say before the Passover event took place. Various late antique chronologists calculated March 29th as the date of Passover moon in the year AD 5502, the first year of creation as determined through the summation of the patriarchs' ages as described in Genesis 5 (for example, "When Seth had lived 105 years, he fathered Enosh. . . . When Enosh had lived 90 years, he fathered Kenan. . . . When Kenan had lived 70 years, he fathered Mahalalel," and so forth) combined with extrabiblical histories which take over beyond the persons and timeframes given in Scripture. Beginning with the March 25 date for the Annunciation,

Hippolytus assumed—as was common in antiquity and late antiquity—that a nine-month gestation period was ideal[13] and thus December 25 was the date of Christ's birth.

But if arguments drawn from Scripture and history are not persuasive in showing March 25th was the first day of creation, there are poetic arguments, as well.

March 25th is the date of the vernal equinox, at least so far as the date was determined by the Roman calendar. On the vernal equinox, day and night are perfectly balanced with one another. While contemporary Christians are quick to dismiss the possibility of such a day having any meaning, early Christians understood the day as a sign of God's perfect order. The vernal equinox revealed a God Who created the world at an even keel, on a straight line. From a state of equal day and equal night, the days would grow longer as the plan of God unfolded and the knowledge of God grew in the City of God, which was first comprised of the angels but expanded later to include mankind. In

---

13. Ibid., 549.

all this, a profound argument emerges in favor of human personhood beginning at conception, an argument which began long before modern discoveries about the fertilization of eggs. While Christ was born on December 25th, the Incarnation did not occur then. The Incarnation took place on the day the Word became flesh, March 25th, the date of the Annunciation. On the first March 25th, God began revealing Himself through creation, and on a later March 25th, He fulfilled the promises He had begun on that first day. This symmetry reveals the character of a God for Whom all things are appointed perfectly. New Testament scholars like Peter Leithart and Dale Allison have spent significant portions of their careers showing how the Gospel writers conceived of Christ not only as the Second Adam, but as the Second Moses, the Second David, the Second Solomon, even the Second Hebrew Nation. Everything within the sacred history of Yahweh and His people pointed toward Jesus Christ, Whose life was the great and final fulfillment of all that God had ever begun doing. In this way, Christ is not simply the Second Adam or the Second Moses. He is the Second and final "let there be light."

Defamers of the December 25 date often suggest that Christians selected their date for Christ's birth out of jealousy for the celebration of Saturnalia, a pagan festival which occurred around the same time. If the December 25 date for Christ's birth had not arisen until the fifth or sixth century AD, this argument might rise to the level of warranting a response; however, the idea that Christians of the late second century were jealous of pagans could only be held by someone who is staggeringly ignorant of history.

To begin with, there is a vast chasm which separates the earliest Christian claims that Christ was born on December 25th and the earliest celebrations of Christmas. For Julius Africanus and Hippolytus, the fact that Christ was born on December 25th was simply a matter of fact, an historical and theological claim as *culturally* benign as the fact that Christ was left behind in Jerusalem when He was twelve. At the time when December 25th was established by Hippolytus as the date of Christ's birthday, most Christians (probably including Hippolytus himself) regarded the celebration of birthdays as a thing only pagans did. The idea that the December 25 date was chosen by Christians as part of a cultural operation to overtake Saturnalia assumes Christians were willing to *celebrate* Christ's birth almost two centuries before they were willing to do so. The celebration of Christmas as a church feast day, attended by distinct liturgical operations of the church, did not come about until Hippolytus had been dead for some time.

Consider also that when Hippolytus and Africanus wrote, Christians were being persecuted by the Roman state. Hippolytus was ultimately martyred for Christ. The love which underwrites martyrdom is a love which cannot be tempted by the things of this earth. Is it reasonable to claim that this same Hippolytus was looking longingly at the things of the same Roman state that tortured his teachers, his friends, and which would ultimately slaughter him? If contemporary Christians believe that the December 25 date was chosen out of jealousy for paganism, it seems they are actually projecting their own neuroses on

Christians of a bygone era who could look on the things of the world without desire, unlike ourselves, for Christians now lust zealously after every jot and tittle of the secularist cultural program. Christians want their music to sound like the world's music. Christians no longer name their churches after saints, but night clubs. Christians want to dress like their atheist contemporaries. They want to take over Hollywood and Nashville. They do not contemplate martyrdom as a serious possibility and so they cannot believe that Christians have ever done anything other than bow to the whims and tastes of those who hate God. They assume that the age of martyrs was stocked with people as shallow as themselves.

Besides, Christians of the second and third centuries AD had no desire to overtake Saturnalia because they did not believe the world would last very long. Prior to the Edict of Milan, the overwhelming majority of Christians waited eagerly, daily for the Lord's return, expecting it would be "any day now." Apocalyptic literature which reads like the book of Revelation was quite common during the second century. In fact, the book of Revelation was one of the last books in the New Testament to be canonized because there was such an abundance of obscurantist dream literature about the end of the world being circulated at the time when the canon was being debated. It was not until the middle of the fourth century AD when Christians adjusted their expectations, refined their theology, and concluded the Earth would be around for a while, that anything resembling a modern cultural program came together within the church, and by this time, the December 25 date was fixed in the East and West alike.

Finally, December 25th was the Roman date for the winter solstice, the shortest and darkest day of the year. Christ is the final "let there be light," and yet His light remained hidden in Mary's womb for nine months. From the day Christ's face first shines on creation, the world becomes increasingly bright. Christ is the Light Who enlightens all men, and once that light emerges from the darkness of the womb, the knowledge of God grows in man. Thus, the December 25 date reveals a symmetry and harmony between heaven and earth. As the heavens become enlightened, so does mankind. The harmony of heaven and earth are embodied in Christ Himself, Who is both God and Man, first and last, finite and infinite, bounded and boundless.

The claims that Christ was born "sometime in August or September" and that Christmas was "originally Saturnalia" are often presented as though they are born of genuine research and a respect for historicity when they are anything but. Even the coy defamer of the traditional date who claims it would have been "too cold" for shepherds to keep watch over their flocks by night out on the hills cannot be troubled to do a simple Google search for Bethlehem weather on the evening of December 24. I have been checking every year now for nearly a decade and can happily report Bethlehem is usually in the upper 50s to lower 60s F on Christmas Eve. The average American puts on a light jacket for such temperatures.

And so I think it fair to say that Christmas is exactly what it has always purported to be: the timely celebration of Jesus Christ's birth, wherein everyone is more generous than usual because heaven and earth have drawn close together and, accordingly, the economies of divine love hold greater sway over our hearts. Christmas does not need us. We need Christmas. Christmas is not a holiday that ought to be celebrated tepidly and apprehensively, as though an embarrassing pratfall awaits the man who uncritically gives himself over to it. Christmas will not be understood and enjoyed more thoroughly by the man who approaches it with a skeptical spirit, on guard for tricks and delusions of the superstitious. A generation beholden to fast food, reality television, pornography, free money, celebrity newscasters, pointless wars, and blockbuster films simply has very little idea about what sort of things actually deserve skepticism. Instead, Christmas ought to be celebrated deeply and faithfully, with the full confidence that our Christian ancestors knew that it was not just right to preserve the December 25 date, but *pious*.

Death at a Party

December 28th Feast of the Holy Innocents

Because I teach high school literature, I can take the end of the year off, set aside my books, my labor, and everything that *must* be done. The week between Christmas and New Year's is suspended above and beyond earthly time. This is surplus time. Fat time. Slush hours. Cronos does not know what to do with these days. My children are stuffed with jam and chocolate. I am stuffed with wine and jam and chocolate. And yet, the Feast of the Massacre of the Holy Innocents sits squarely in the middle of this week. In the midst of our celebrations, infant blood.

How can we have so much plenty against the suffering of others? I will buy *The New York Times* on Sunday, open a bottle of Garnacha, and read about how awful life is for most people on planet Earth. The prophets on the opinion page predict the worst for the year to come. The cult of various false gods is slated to finally do us in. The Devil said it. I fear it. That settles it. Christ comes on the darkest day of the year, and from that point forward the days grow longer, but don't make too much of it, yet. We are not allowed to remember the dead Innocents before Christmas and get them out of the way. Their feast day comes on the fourth day of Christmas. In the middle of dinner, the dead children come to the door. The dead knock between toasts to life. We peer out the glass window, but it is fogged over, and when we open the door, they lay in piles on our front porch. The Christ has come with a price.

The Holy Innocents prepare us for the next coming feast day, which is not devoted to Christ, but to Janus, the god who saw the past and the future and recognized little disparity between the two: dead infants in their time, dead infants in our time. The murder of the guiltless is an ancient human preoccupation. We get fidgety and the good die. Every newspaper now comes with a story on the fourth or fifth page about a man who murdered his family last night. Our day and age is every day and age.

We know that Christmas is somehow solemn, but Americans are at a loss for talking about the Holy Innocents. They intrude into our triumph with their pathetic failure to live. We have tried to celebrate them during the Advent fast, but they refuse to be honored during times of leanness. *We will only be known during times of gold and perfume, they say. We have borne the brunt of the war on Christmas, they say, and do not care for your cool dismissals.*

The blues descend upon us during Christmas, though we do not know why. Christmas is come, and we want for dead things and suffering things. *It is only right to be sad*, we say, though we do not know why.

In the fat time between Christmas and New Year's, we must make room for the Holy Innocents. We need an hour to listen to Faure's *Requiem* and imagine we are the dead, traversing each of the seven movements like spheres of the heavens until we are delivered into the Empyrean. We need the darkness to crowd out the light for a moment. We need these long, empty, meandering afternoons to think of nothing on behalf of those who never knew. We need the butterscotch to sour in our mouths just a little, the sweet milk to curdle, the apples to oxidize brown and unpicturesque for the sake of those cut down before their time. The Christ did not come for free. The little children joined Abel and bought Him to us.

We do not know what to say to the Holy Innocents, so we say nothing and complain of Christmas blues. We sense amid the celebration that some who ought to be with us are not present. We know that our joy can only be complete by ceremonially acknowledging that it is incomplete. We know that, soon enough, the tree will be stripped naked and burned. We know that January is the month fitness clubs make all their money, as the fatness is taken back by a want for leanness, sleekness, nothingness. The party will soon drain from our flesh, and if it will not, so much the worse for our spirits.

In the days of fatness, the days of surplus eternity, make room for the living Christ in your life, and make room for the dead Innocents. Do not forget the heavy cost of the Incarnation. Christ shared His glory with the Holy Innocents, just as He shares His glory with anyone who "lays down his life" for his friend. Christ shares His glory with the slaughtered, those who died "before their time," and we must share our glory with them, as well.

The Leavetaking

Even when Christmas has been celebrated properly, with a good month of renunciation leading up to the 25th and twelve solid days of feasting thereafter, returning back to the normal run of things may nonetheless prove disheartening. The English poet W.H. Auden captured the bleakness of early January in the closing moments of *For the Time Being: A Christmas Oratorio*, a lengthy dramatic work comprised of a series of monologues by various figures related to the Christmas story. Since the original performance of For the Time Being in 1944, the conclusion of Auden's work has proven the most resilient and famous passage, whereby it is often performed or recited independently of the rest of the *Oratorio*.

The final sixty lines of *For the Time Being* look back at the celebration of Christmas from an outsider's perspective and highlight a host of important truths which are easy to miss while in the middle of things. To begin with, Christmas is a holiday typically celebrated with family, regardless of what one thinks of his family. When one conceives of Christmas primarily as a pleasant thing, as opposed to a holy thing, it is easy to think that family gets in the way of Christmas, when the opposite is true. Celebrating Christmas with family often involves travel, which is both costly and risky in the winter, and if pleasure is all one wants from Christmas, travel for the sake of family is both needlessly expensive and counterproductive. Why not spend Christmas with friends, people we choose to love simply because we love the same things? *Some* people find their families easy to love, but most do not, for our families are *our own* whether they agree with our political opinions or not, and most do not, which means that family Christmas typically segues, at some point or another, into acrimony and disagreement. However, Auden helplessly places blame for this acrimony on himself and his "gross [overestimation]" of his own charitable instincts. His relatives are contentious, but not more contentious than himself, and he confesses that any difficulties associated with family Christmas represent his own inability to love his aunts, uncles, and cousins with the same generosity with which Christ loves all mankind. Which is greater: the disparity between Christ and ourselves, or the disparity between ourselves and our idiot relations? Thus, when the time comes to depart from our relatives, if we are struck by just how much we do not get along, we would do well to recall all the ways in which we have attempted to exploit Christ throughout the year and not to dwell on all those ways our relatives have tried to exploit us, the state, or our churches. We visit our relatives not because it is fun (though it is, sometimes), but as a reminder of Christ's infinite condescension in leaving His Father to caravan with the same beings who created crucifixion, *Penthouse* magazine, abstract expressionism, and atomic weapons. What appears below is quite a long quote of poetry. Perhaps revisit copyright law in this case. From my research, as of 2020 only works published prior to 1924 and works whose author died before 1951 are in the public domain.

Visiting our families at Christmas is an act of faith, a pilgrimage, then, for it reminds us that in the same way we plead with God to have mercy on us because we are "the work of His hands," we are also, to a lesser extent, the work of our ancestors' hands, and we need their love and clemency, even when they are hard to love, for we are also hard to love, as is God Himself often hard to love.

Auden's poem also presents us with the paradox of Christmas, for in the midst of our sensual enjoyment of so many good things, we cannot fail to recognize that God made us for something other than raw sensuality. It is easier to understand the limits of sensual pleasure while surrounded by it than when looking forward to it. Thus, during an ascetic Advent one recognizes the limits of pleasure, even while anticipating it, and during the twelve days of Christmas one enjoys pleasure, even while recognizing its ultimate insufficiency. During Christmas, many "see the actual vision," which is to say that in the midst of all the tiresome preparations and the parties, there is at least one full minute in which true Christians are confronted with the profundity of the Incarnation, the extreme humility of Jesus Christ, and they are cut to the heart. The meaning of Christmas lays bare just how much of our lives are spent serving ourselves, pleasing ourselves, and evading responsibility for our sins, and yet, God became man that man may become God, as St. Athanasius famously put it. Nonetheless, we have resisted God's call to become like Him, we have not "set our minds on things above," and for a single, fleeting moment on Christmas Eve, while holding a candle and singing "O, Come All Ye Faithful," a man wishes he had anonymously given gifts to his enemies, wishes that he had spent more on his wife, wishes that he had given more of himself away—to the poor, to God. Perhaps this revelation will not just last the evening, but a whole week, and yet Auden soberly directs his attention to the moment the revelation melts, solid life returns, and we must resume living in "for the time being."

"The time being" is the normal world, the secular world, the world wherein no great spiritual truth is being unveiled for us. Hitting "the time being" feels a good bit like stepping off a moving sidewalk in an airport, for all the spiritual progress we have made in the wake of "the actual vision" is sublimated by the realization that "the streets / Are much narrower," which is to say we have put on eight pounds since the 25th and having three drinks every evening is no longer excusable.

The Greek sage Hesiod once said, "At the beginning of a cask and at the end take your fill; in the middle be sparing," and early January resumes the sparing middle portion of life, the portion where nothing pleasant waits in the wings. God is not in the habit of creating things holy. He creates them common, then, through a series of rituals and ceremonies, common things become holy. Common things and holy things are not the opposites of one another, neither are common things bad. Common things are simply lesser goods, lesser visions of God, and yet, moving from the holy back to the common is a shock, for the world seems drained of meaning, plain, and dreadfully blank. When we move from the holy to the common (from the beginning of the cask to the middle), our senses are numb, which means we are stuck all day in the company of our souls, and our souls are like old men who are constantly recalling our failures to us. Accordingly, "We look round for something, no matter what, to inhibit / Our self-reflection," which often means going back to the bottle when what we really need, according to Auden, is "some great suffering," some fresh renunciation, some terrible project (sandbagging the levee), some selfless labor which will help us quit thinking of ourselves. The suffering "will come, all right," and before the end of January, some new scandal will have arisen, some new plague, some new ambiguous pain near our left kidney which Google suggests might be cancer, and all the grey blankness of January will vanish in a flurry of honest prayers and painful confessions.

Until then, though, it is our place to redeem the Time Being "from insignificance." The Time Being is "noon," the hot and pointless part of the day during which the demon Acedia calls us from our work to something more interesting, more fun, more profitable. This is the time when "the Spirit must practice his scales of rejoicing / Without even a hostile audience," which is to suggest the arid meaninglessness of January is largely our own faults, for we have quit frequenting church. On Christmas and Easter, we pray happily. While awaiting test results, we pray sadly (or accusingly). Between, though, we pray very little. Thus, Auden's poem concludes with a pious call to adventure. January is not the month to make a deal with a gym, but the month to make a deal with God. The thin, atheistic shallows of the year cannot be drunk away, cannot be sweated out, cannot find their end in self-care. Instead, we must "Follow Him," "Seek Him," and "Love Him." God makes Himself easy to see at Christmas, and though we may find Him in the dregs of Winter, we will have to find Him in "the Kingdom of Anxiety," in nearly empty vespers services, during tasteless meals thrown together to make room for sudden avalanches of work, as the credit card bills for December roll in.

It is for such moments that Christ came.

Bibliography

"The Angels Wanna Wear My Red Suit." *This American Life* episode 148. December 24, 1999.

Aristotle. *Rhetoric*. Translated by W. Rhys Roberts. Mineola, NY: Dover, 2004.

Augustine, Saint. *The City of God*. Translated by Marcus Dodds. Peabody, MA: Hendrickson Publishers, 2009.

Gregory of Nyssa, Saint. *The Life of Moses*. Translated by Abraham J. Malherbe, Everett Ferguson. Mahwah NJ: Paulist Press, 1978.

Grout, James. "Sol Invictus and Christmas." Encyclopedia Romana. Accessed August 22, 2020. https://penelope.uchicago.edu/~grout/encyclopaedia_romana/calendar/invictus.html.

Hart, David Bentley. *The Beauty of the Infinite: The Aesthetics of Christian Truth*. Grand Rapids: Eerdmans, 2004.

Hijmans, Steven. "Sol Invictus, the Winter Solstice, and the Origins of Christmas." *Mouseion* 47.3 (2003) 377–398.

Reno, R.R. "Fighting the Noonday Devil." *First Things*, August 2003.

Schmidt, Thomas C. "Calculating December 25 as the Birth of Jesus in Hippolytus' *Canon and Chronicon.*" *Vigiliae Christianae* 69.5 (2015) 542–63.

"The Scots Demonstration of their Abhorrence of Popery, with all its Adherents in a Letter from Edenbrough to a Friend in London, Containing the Manner of Burning the Pope There in Essigie, on Christ Mass Day. &C." Accessed August 19, 2020. The National Library of Scotland.
https://natlib.govt.nz/records/20632894?-search%5Bi%5D%5Bcentury%5D=1600&search%-5Bi%5 D%5Bdecade%5D=1670&search%5B-path%5D=items.